THE BEST AND BIGGEST FUN WORK BOOK

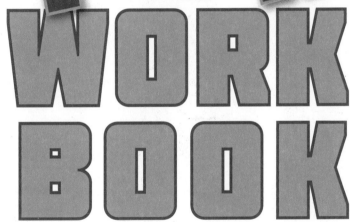

FOR MINECRAFTERS

Grades 1 & 2

Illustrated by Amanda Brack

Sky Pony Press
New York

Copyright © 2019 by Hollan Publishing, Inc.

Minecraft® is a registered trademark of Notch Development AB.

The Minecraft game is copyright © Mojang AB.

Sky Pony Press books may be purchased in bulk at special discounts for sales promotion, corporate gifts, fund-raising, or educational purposes. Special editions can also be created to specifications. For details, contact the Special Sales Department, Sky Pony Press, 307 West 36th Street, 11th Floor, New York, NY 10018 or info@skyhorsepublishing.com.

Sky Pony® is a registered trademark of Skyhorse Publishing, Inc.®, a Delaware corporation.

Minecraft® is a registered trademark of Notch Development AB.
The Minecraft game is copyright © Mojang AB.

Visit our website at www.skyponypress.com.

Authors, books, and more at SkyPonyPressBlog.com.

10 9 8 7 6 5 4 3 2 1

Cover design by Brian Peterson

Puzzles created by Jen Funk Weber

Interior art by Amanda Brack

Book design by Kevin Baier

Print ISBN: 978-1-5107-4496-7

Printed in China

A NOTE TO PARENTS

Welcome to a great big world of fun and learning with a Minecrafting twist. When you want to reinforce classroom skills, break up screen time, or enhance kids' problem-solving skills at home, it's crucial to have high-interest, kid-friendly learning materials.

The Best and Biggest Fun Workbook for Minecrafters transforms educational lessons into exciting adventures complete with diamond swords, zombies, skeletons, and creepers. With colorful illustrations and familiar characters to guide them through, your kids will feel like winners from start to finish.

This mega-fun workbook is organized into six distinct chapters targeting a wide variety of math, problem-solving, and language arts skills. Inside you'll find exercises in math basics like skip counting; mazes, games, and puzzles that help develop problem-solving skills; guided instruction for writing the alphabet; and reading activities designed to boost fluency. Use the table of contents to pinpoint areas for extra practice!

Now for the best part: The educational content in this workbook is aligned with National Common Core Standards for first and second grade. What does that mean, exactly? Everything in this book matches up with what your children are learning or will be learning in first and second grade. This eliminates confusion, builds confidence, and keeps them ahead of the curve.

Whether it's the joy of seeing their favorite game come to life on each page or the thrill of solving challenging problems just like Steve and Alex, there is something in *The Best and Biggest Fun Workbook for Minecrafters* to entice every student.

Happy adventuring!

# CONTENTS

Math for Minecrafters

Addition, Subtraction, and More!..................... 5
Answer Key 50

Word Problems 55
Answer Key 104

Math Facts.. 109
Answer Key 146

Games and Puzzles for Minecrafters

Amazing Activities 153
Answer Key 220

Language Arts for Minecrafters

Printing Practice 231

Reading 293
Answer Key 350

MATH FOR MINECRAFTERS

ADDITION, SUBTRACTION, AND MORE!

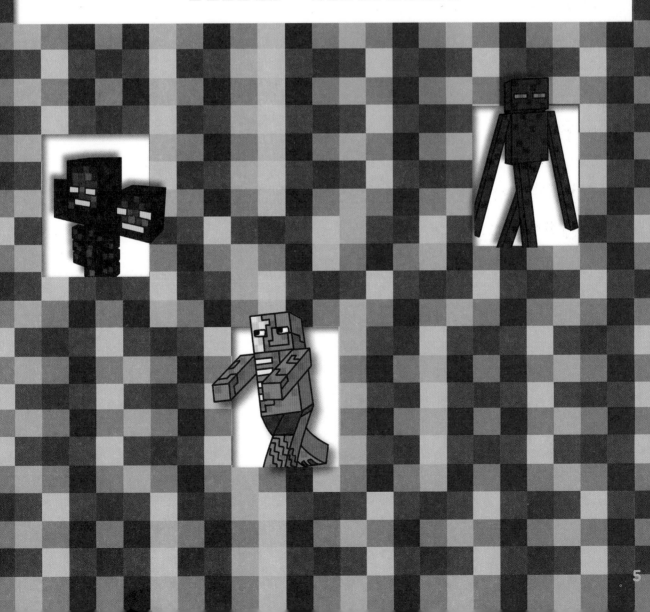

ADDITION BY GROUPING

Circle groups of 10. Then count and write the total numbers.

Example:

1.

Answer: 26

2.

Answer: _____

3.

Answer: _____

4.

Answer: _____

5.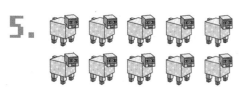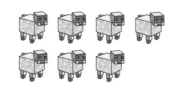

Answer: _____

MYSTERY MESSAGE
WITH ADDITION
AND SUBTRACTION

Add or subtract. Then use the letters to fill in the blanks below and reveal the answer to Steve's joke.

1. 4 + 8 = 12 S   6. 8 – 2 = ___ R

2. 6 – 3 = ___ N   7. 9 + 6 = ___ B

3. 3 + 8 = ___ T   8. 10 – 3 = ___ L

4. 7 – 5 = ___ M   9. 5 + 9 = ___ E

5. 8 + 5 = ___ A

Q: Why do Minecraft horses eat golden apples and carrots with their mouths open?

A: Because they have bad...

COPY THE LETTERS FROM THE ANSWERS ABOVE TO SOLVE THE MYSTERY.

S ___ ___ ___ ___ ___
12   11   13   15   7   14

___ ___ ___ ___ ___ ___ S
2   13   3   3   14   6   12

ZOMBIE'S GUIDE TO PLACE VALUE

Use the number on each zombie to fill in the place-value chart. Then, write the number in tally marks.

Example: **1.**

Tens	Ones
3	6

‖‖‖ ‖‖‖   ‖‖‖ |
‖‖‖ ‖‖‖
‖‖‖ ‖‖‖

2.

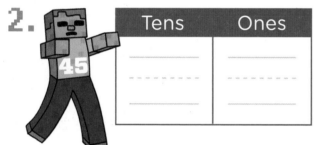

Tens	Ones

3.

Tens	Ones

4.

Tens	Ones

5.

Tens	Ones

6.

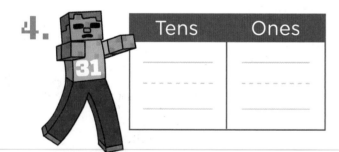

Tens	Ones

7.

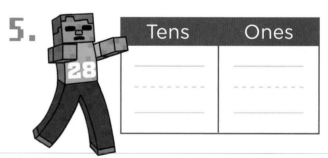

Tens	Ones

SKIP COUNT CHALLENGE

Count by 2s and fill in the empty spaces to keep Alex at a safe distance from the cave spider.

2 — 4 — 6

26

TELLING TIME

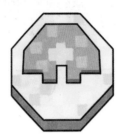

Look at the clocks below and write the time in the space provided.

Example:

1.

Answer:  2:00

2.

Answer: _____

3.

Answer: _____

4.

Answer: _____

5.

Answer: _____

6.

Answer: _____

COUNTING MONEY

The villagers are letting you trade coins for emeralds.
Add up your coins to see how much money you have.

25¢   10¢   5¢   1¢

1. 25¢ + 10¢ + 10¢ + 5¢ = **50** ¢

2. 10¢ + 5¢ + 5¢ + 1¢ + 1¢ + 1¢ = _____

3. 25¢ + 10¢ + 1¢ = _____

4. 25¢ + 25¢ + 5¢ + 5¢ = _____

5. 10¢ + 10¢ + 10¢ + 5¢ + 1¢ + 1¢ = _____

6. 25¢ + 5¢ + 5¢ + 5¢ + 1¢ = _____

7. 5¢ + 1¢ + 1¢ + 1¢ + 1¢ = _____

HARDCORE MODE: *Try this hardcore math challenge!*

8. One villager charges 25¢ for each emerald. How many (5¢) nickels do you need in order to buy an emerald?

Answer: _____

ADVENTURES IN GEOMETRY

Let's learn about fractions! Count the number of squares in the crafting grid below.

Example: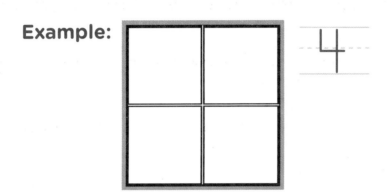

1. Color one of the four squares brown.

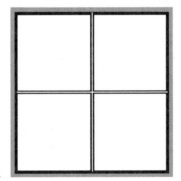

This is called one fourth, or ¼.

2. This crafting grid is divided into two equal parts. Color one of the two parts brown.

This is called one half, or ½.

3. Count the rectangles in the experience bar below.
Write the number here: _____

4. This experience bar is divided into three equal parts.
Color one part green.

This is called one third, or ⅓.

5. This experience bar is divided into three equal parts.
Color two parts green.

This is called two thirds, or ⅔.

HARDCORE MODE: *Try this hardcore math challenge!*
A health bar can show up to 10 hearts. Color in 5 hearts below.

Circle the fraction that describes how many are colored in:

A. 1/2   **B.** 1/4   **C.** 1/3

WORD PROBLEMS

Read the problem carefully. Use the picture to help you solve the problem. Fill in your answer.

Example:

You get 10 minutes of daylight in Minecraft. You lose 8 minutes building a shelter and finding food. How many minutes are left?

X	X	X	X	X	X	X	X		

10 – 8 =   *2*

Answer: *2 minutes*

1. You need 4 wooden planks to make a crafting table, but you only have 3. How many more planks do you need?

Answer: _____

2. There are 9 empty spaces in your inventory bar. You fill 4 spaces with tools. How many empty spaces do you have?

Answer: _____

3. 7 green experience orbs appear. You collect 3 of them. How many orbs are left to collect?

Answer: _____

4. You have 6 sheep on your farm. You add 2 pigs to the farm. How many animals do you have?

Answer: _____

5. You have 7 blocks of sandstone. You get 4 more blocks. How many blocks of sandstone do you have?

Answer: _____

6. 8 creepers are chasing you. 2 of them blow up! How many creepers are still chasing you?

Answer: _____

7. Alex has 7 potions in her inventory. She crafts 2 more potions. How many potions does she have?

Answer: _____

8. Yesterday you attacked 5 zombie pigmen. Today you attacked 8. How many more pigmen did you attack today than yesterday?

Answer: _____

GHAST'S GUIDE TO PLACE VALUE

Read the number on each ghast to fill in the place-value chart. Then, write the number in tally marks.

Example:

1.  26

Tens	Ones
2	6

|||| |||| ||| |
|||| ||||

2. 43

Tens	Ones

3. 35

Tens	Ones

4. 29

Tens	Ones

5. 47

Tens	Ones

6. 89

Tens	Ones

7. 63

Tens	Ones

SKIP COUNT CHALLENGE

Steve is tired after a long day of mining. Count by 5s and fill in the spaces to help him get home on his new railway system.

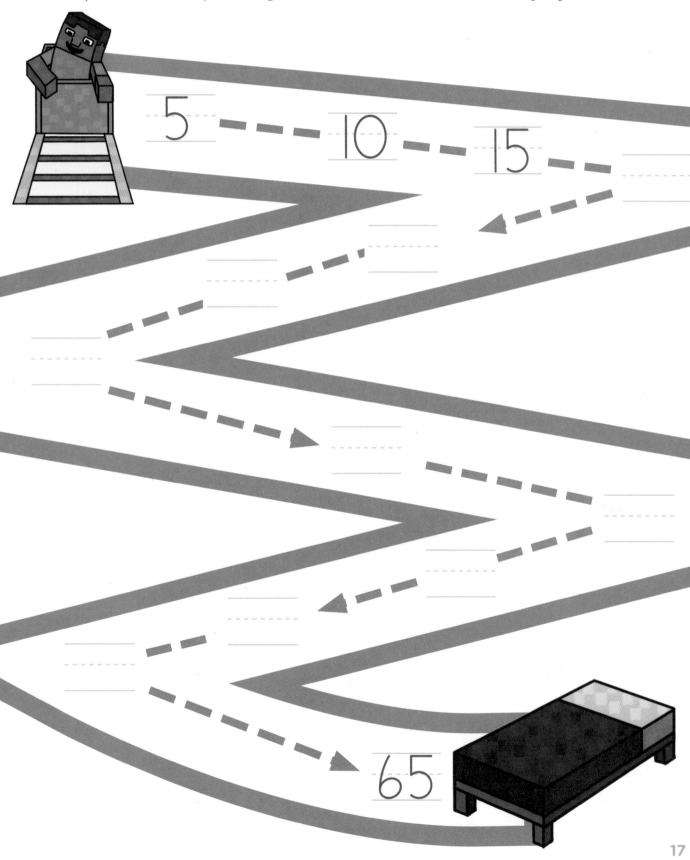

5 — 10 — 15 — ___

65

ALL IN A DAY'S WORK

A minecrafter's first day is very busy!
Match the time for each task on the left with a clock on the right.

1.  **6:00** Smash a tree to get wood.

2. **7:30** Make a pickaxe.

3.  **9:00** Get some wool.

4. 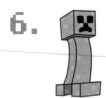 **10:00** Build a bed.

5.  **2:30** Build a shelter.

6. **8:00** Hear a creeper hiss nearby.

7. **8:30** Build a door fast. Phew!

A.

B.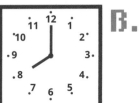

C.

D.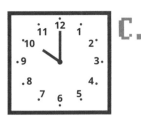

E.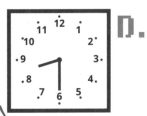

F.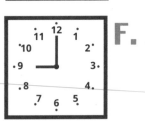

G.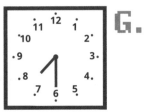

TIME FOR MATCHING

Draw a big hand and a little hand on the clock to show the time.

Example:

1.

3:00

2.
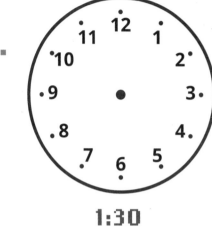
1:30

3.
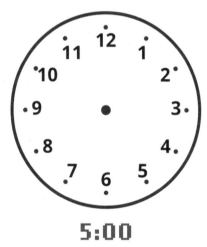
5:00

4.
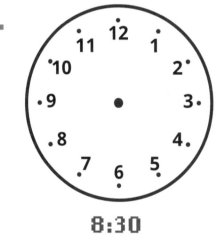
8:30

5.
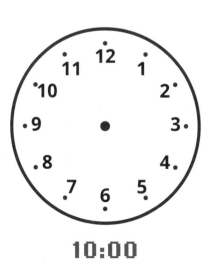
10:00

6.
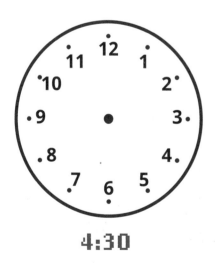
4:30

LEARNING ABOUT SHAPES

Draw along the dotted line to complete each shape. Connect the name of the shape to the correct drawing.

1. rectangle

A.

2. square

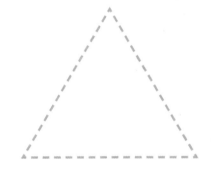

B.

3. trapezoid

C.

4. triangle

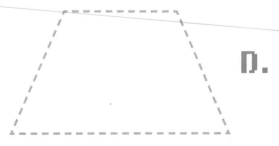

D.

FIND THE SHAPES

Look at the items below and and use the word box to write the name.

square	circle	rectangle

5.

_____

6.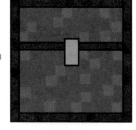

_____

7.

_____

8. HARDCORE MODE: *Try this hardcore math challenge!*
Find 6 rectangles in this bottle of potion.

ADDITION BY GROUPING

Circle groups of 10 weapons and tools. Then count and write the total number.

Example:

1.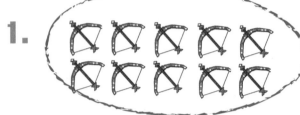

Answer: 16

2.

Answer: _____

3.

Answer: _____

4.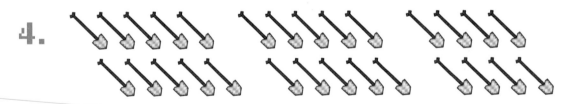

Answer: _____

5.

Answer: _____

MYSTERY MESSAGE
WITH ADDITION AND SUBTRACTION

Add or subtract. Then use the letters to fill in the blanks below and reveal the answer to Steve's joke.

1. $12 + 8 = 20$ H

2. $16 + 3 =$ E

3. $11 - 8 =$ A

4. $19 - 5 =$ B

5. $14 + 3 =$ Y

6. $16 + 2 =$ N

7. $20 - 7 =$ T

8. $18 - 3 =$ D

9. $13 - 2 =$ W

10. $17 - 9 =$ O

11. $15 - 8 =$ I

12. $12 + 4 =$ G

Q: Why didn't the skeleton go to Alex's party?

COPY THE LETTERS FROM THE ANSWERS ABOVE TO FIND OUT.

H ___   H ___   ___   ___   ___
20 19   20   3   15   18   8

___   ___   ___   ___   ___   ___
14   8   15   17   13   8

___   ___   ___   ___   ___   H
16   8   11   7   13   20

THE ENDERMAN NUMBER CHALLENGE

Match the Enderman with the description of the number.

1.

Tens	Ones
8	4

2.

Tens	Ones
6	3

3.

Tens	Ones
5	9

4.

Tens	Ones
2	7

5.

Tens	Ones
7	2

A. 27

B. 59

C. 72

D. 84

E. 63

SKIP COUNT CHALLENGE

Count by 10s to help tame the ocelot. Feed it enough fish on this numbered path and you'll have a new pet!

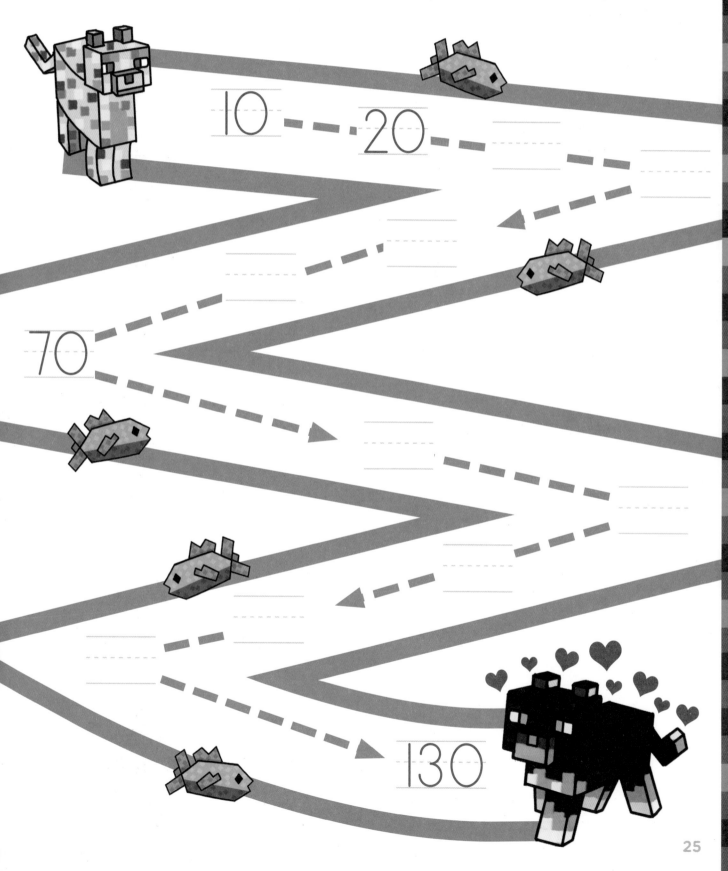

10 ----- 20

70

130

THE TALLEST TOWER

Steve built three watchtowers in different sizes to help him find his way home. Compare the towers and write your answers below.

How many blocks tall is each tower?

A.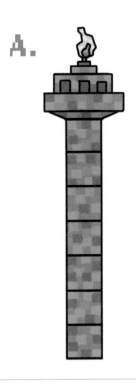

B.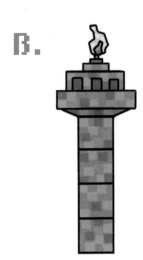

C.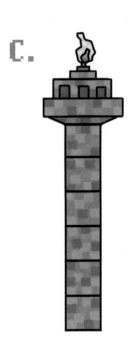

_____   _____   _____

1. Which watchtower is the tallest? _____

2. Which watchtower is the shortest? _____

3. How much taller is watchtower A compared to watchtower B?

_____ **blocks.**

4. Draw your own watchtower, called watchtower D, in the space below. It must be taller than tower B, but shorter than tower C. Color it in using your favorite color!

D.

5. How many blocks tall is your watchtower? _____ **blocks.**

6. Fill in the rest of this table to keep track of all the different towers.

Tower	Number of Blocks Tall	Color
A	7	GRAY
B		
C		
D		

ADVENTURES IN GEOMETRY

Trace the dotted line to divide these shapes into two equal parts. Then color one half (½) of the shape.

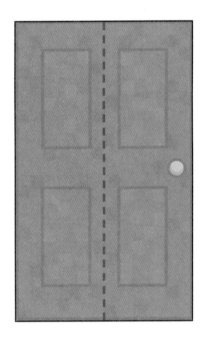

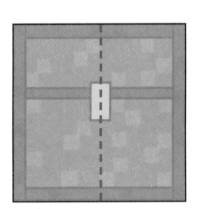

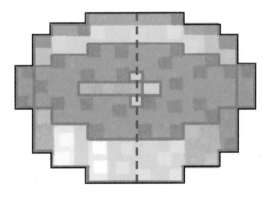

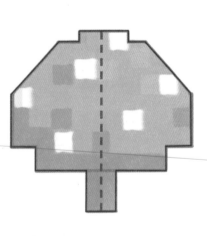

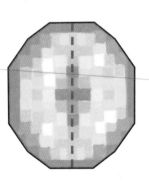

Trace the dotted line to divide these shapes into four equal parts. Then color in one quarter (¼) of each shape below.

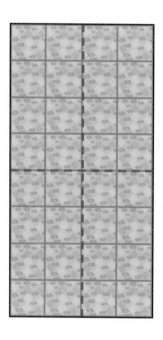

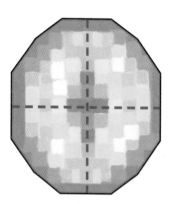

Color in one half of this wooden plank:

½

Color in one quarter of this wooden plank:

¼

WORD PROBLEMS

Read the problem carefully. Look at the picture and fill in your answer.

Example:

1. Steve eats 3 carrots. He attacks zombies, and they drop 2 more carrots and 2 potatoes for him to eat. How many food items does he eat all together?

$$3 + 2 + 2 = 7$$

Answer: 7

2. Alex gets 2 blocks of lava from a blacksmith's house, 5 more from the Nether, and 6 from an End Portal room. How many blocks of lava does she get in all?

Answer: _____

3. Steve sees 16 ghasts on his adventures. He destroys 4 with enchanted arrows and 3 more with fireballs. How many ghasts are left?

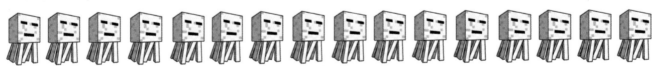

Answer: _____

4. In one day, Steve makes 10 pickaxes, 3 axes, and 9 shovels to attack mobs. How many weapons did he make in all?

Answer: _____

5. Alex gets 6 cookies from trading with a villager. She gets 7 more cookies later in the day and 4 more cookies in the morning. How many cookies does she have in all?

Answer: _____

6. You start your game with 20 hunger points. You lose 2 points running away from a creeper. You lose 4 more points attacking skeletons. How many hunger points are left?

Answer: _____

7. You start your game with 9 items in your inventory. You remove 4 tools and 2 food items. How many items are left in your inventory?

Answer: _____

8. Steve loves his pet cats. He has 4 in a fenced area outside, 7 in his house, and 5 in another fenced area. How many pet cats does he have?

Answer: _____

CREEPER'S GUIDE TO PLACE VALUE

Use the number on each creeper to fill in the place-value chart.

Example:

1.  **354**

Hundreds	Tens	Ones
3	5	4

2.  **760**

Hundreds	Tens	Ones

3.  **592**

Hundreds	Tens	Ones

4.  **184**

Hundreds	Tens	Ones

5. **532**

Hundreds	Tens	Ones

6.  **956**

Hundreds	Tens	Ones

7.  **453**

Hundreds	Tens	Ones

SKIP COUNT CHALLENGE

Fill in the blank spaces as you count from 110 to 125 and help Alex find her way back to her house.

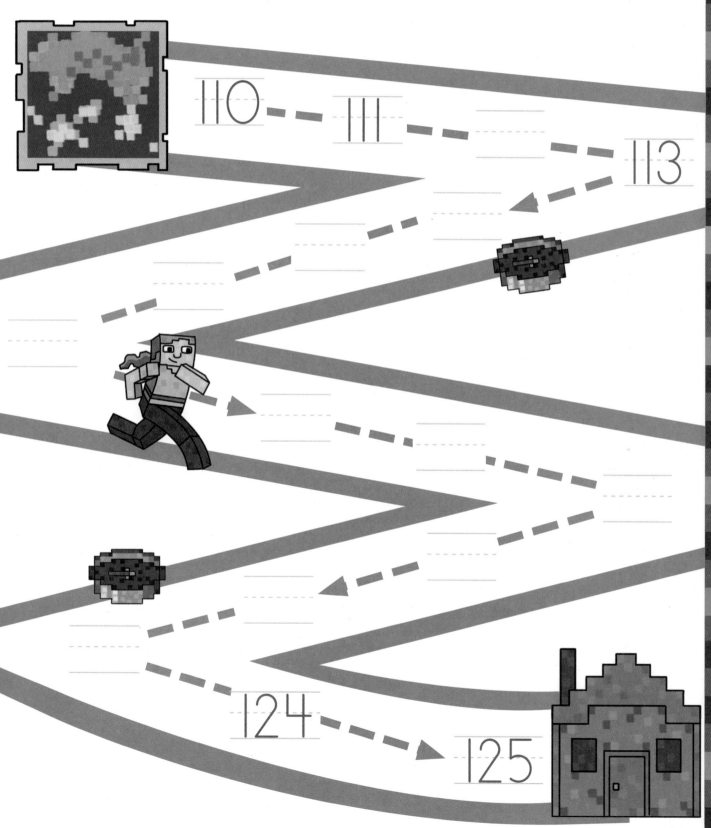

110 — — 111 — — — — 113

124 — — — 125

MOBS AND MONSTERS

Video game characters are sometimes called mobs. Add an X to the boxes that describe each mob in the table below.

	Creeper	Zombie	Ghast	Enderman	Cave Spider	Snow Golem
0 Legs						
2 Legs						
More than 2 Legs						

Use the table to answer these questions.

1. How many mobs have more than 2 legs? _____

2. How many mobs have 2 legs or less? _____

3. Which 2 mobs are the same color, but have a different number of legs and eyes? _____

COUNTING MONEY

Steve wants to feed his farm animals the following items. Find out how much money each item costs and write the amount in the space provided.

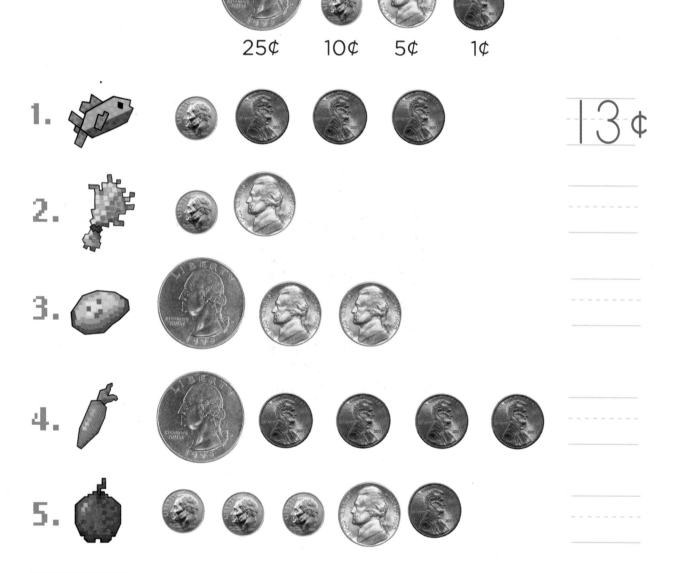

25¢   10¢   5¢   1¢

1.   13¢

2.

3.

4.

5.

HARDCORE MODE: *Try this hardcore math challenge!*

6. How much money does Steve need to buy all five of the food items listed above? Add them up to find out!

Answer:

ADVENTURES IN GEOMETRY: SPOT THE SHAPES

Look at the Minecrafter's house and answer the questions.
Use the shapes below to help you.

rectangle

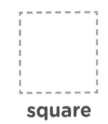

square

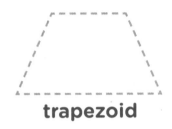

trapezoid

1. What shape is the roof of this house?

2. What shape is the double window?

3. What shape is the doorknob?

CREATIVE MODE

Use a pencil or pen to change the roof into a triangle!

Draw your own Minecrafter's house in the space below. Use as many shapes as you can. Add fun details and color!

SANDSTONE ADDITION

Add the ones and then the tens to get the answer.

1.
$$50 + 26$$
D

2.
$$72 + 25$$
Q

3.
$$43 + 32$$
T

4.
$$20 + 64$$
E

5.
$$82 + 15$$
Z

6.
$$90 + 8$$
S

7.
$$83 + 14$$
M

8.
$$44 + 30$$
E

9.
$$25 + 61$$
R

10.
$$16 + 43$$
B

11.
$$24 + 12$$
T

12.
$$55 + 54$$
K

HIDDEN MESSAGE:

Even numbers end in 0, 2, 4, 6, or 8. Circle the EVEN numbered answers above. Write the letter from those blocks in order from left to right below to spell out the name of a biome with lots of sandstone:

_____ _____ _____

_____ _____ _____

SUBTRACTION MYSTERY MESSAGE

Subtract the ones, then the tens. Use the letters to fill in the blanks below and answer Steve's riddle.

1. 45
  − 32
  _____

  S

2. 89
  − 45
  _____

  C

3. 93
  − 32
  _____

  O

4. 27
  − 12
  _____

  I

5. 32
  − 11
  _____

  U

6. 94
  − 23
  _____

  E

7. 48
  − 37
  _____

  F

8. 74
  − 32
  _____

  R

9. 68
  − 42
  _____

  M

10. 86
  − 33
  _____

  P

Q: What music does a creeper enjoy most?
Copy the letters from the answers above to find out!

____ ____ ____   ____ ____ ____ ____ ____
53   61   53   26   21   13   15   44

____ ____   ____ ____ ____ ____ ____ ____
61   11   44   61   21   42   13   71

MOB MONSTER SHOWDOWN

Who has more attack power? Compare the number of times each mob has attacked a player and write in the correct symbol.

Enderman has more attack power. He wins round 1!

> means greater than   **<** means less than

Example **1.** 385 **<** 392

2. 856   826

3. 445   454

4. 523   527

5. 672   607

6. 908   998

7. 746   772

Count up their wins and circle the one with the most wins below.

Skeleton   **Enderman**

SKIP COUNT CHALLENGE

Count by 3s to collect all of the ink from the squids.

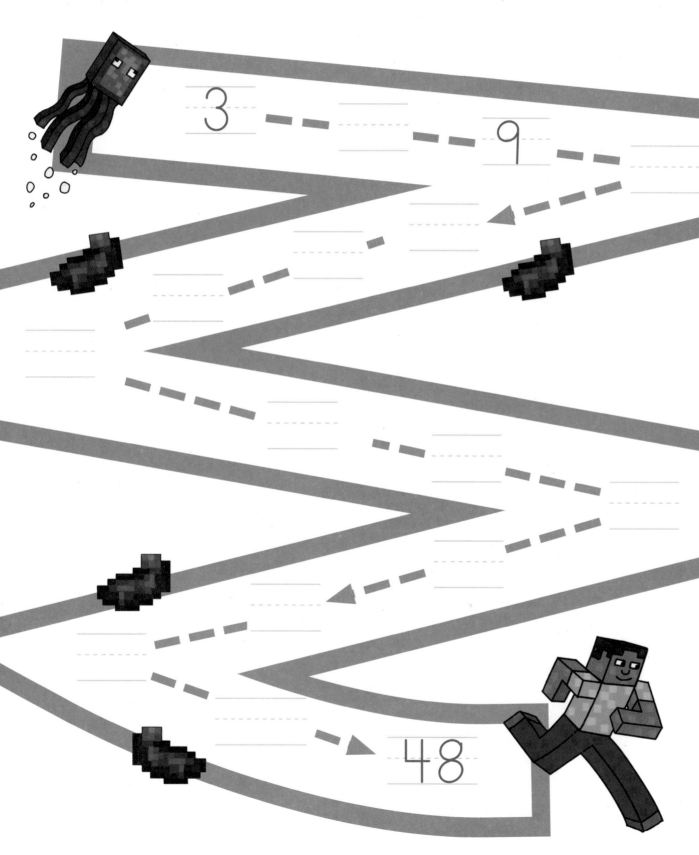

3

9

48

TELLING TIME

Look at the clocks below and write the time in the space provided:

Example:

1.

Answer: 2:45

2.

Answer: _____

3.

Answer: _____

4.

Answer: _____

5.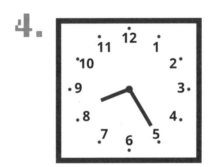

Answer: _____

6.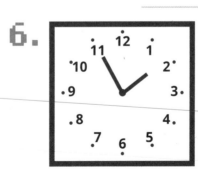

Answer: _____

7.

Answer: _____

8.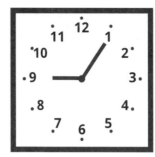

Answer: _____

9.

Answer: _____

10.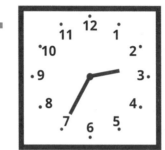

Answer: _____

11.

Answer: _____

12.

Answer: _____

13.

Answer: _____

14.

Answer: _____

4 SIDES ARE BETTER THAN 1

A Minecrafter's world is full of **quadrilaterals**. Find them and circle them below.

Hint: Quadrilaterals are closed shapes with 4 sides. Squares and rectangles are two kinds of quadrilaterals.

Can you find 3 purple quadrilaterals on this fish?

Can you find...
...9 quadrilaterals in this treasure chest?

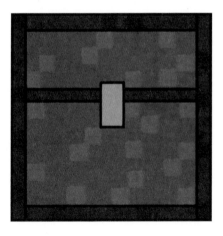

...7 quadrilaterals in this Minecrafter's house?

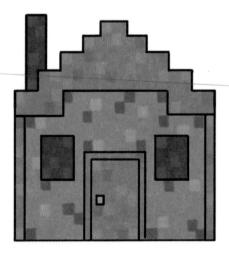

Trace the quadrilaterals below:

ADDITION & SUBTRACTION MYSTERY NUMBER

There is a number hidden behind these redstone blocks.
Subtract or count on to find the mystery number.

1.
$$\begin{array}{r} 15 \\ + \\ \hline 18 \end{array}$$

= 3

2.
$$\begin{array}{r} 22 \\ + \\ \hline 29 \end{array}$$

= _____

3.
$$\begin{array}{r} 43 \\ + \\ \hline 53 \end{array}$$

= _____

4.
$$\begin{array}{r} 17 \\ + \\ \hline 25 \end{array}$$

= _____

5.
$$\begin{array}{r} 76 \\ + \\ \hline 82 \end{array}$$

= _____

6.
$$\begin{array}{r} 50 \\ + \\ \hline 64 \end{array}$$

= _____

7.
$$\begin{array}{r} 49 \\ + \\ \hline 56 \end{array}$$

= _____

8.
$$\begin{array}{r} 27 \\ + \\ \hline 30 \end{array}$$

= _____

9.
$$\begin{array}{r} 63 \\ + \\ \hline 70 \end{array}$$

= _____

MYSTERY MESSAGE
WITH ADDITION USING REGROUPING

Add. Use the letters to fill in the blanks below and answer the riddle.

1. 45
    + 9
    _____

    O

2. 89
    + 7
    _____

    T

3. 33
    + 8
    _____

    N

4. 27
    + 13
    _____

    E

5. 38
    + 6
    _____

    I

6. 25
    + 6
    _____

    F

7. 46
    + 27
    _____

    R

8. 74
    + 19
    _____

    H

9. 28
    + 42
    _____

    S

10. 56
    + 16
    _____

    A

Q: How many pieces of armor can you fit in an empty treasure chest?

54   41   40 .   72   31   96   40   73

96   93   72   96   44   96   70 ,

41   54   96   40   M P   Y .
                                        96

PIGMAN'S GUIDE TO PLACE VALUE

Identify the number that belongs in the place-value chart and write it there.

Example:

1.

5 4

Tens
3

2.

973

Hundreds

3.
462

Ones

4.
875

Hundreds

5.
546

Tens

6.

231

Ones

7.
952

Hundreds

SKIP COUNT CHALLENGE

Enter The End through The End portal and count by 4s until you reach the Enderdragon for an epic battle.

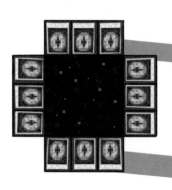

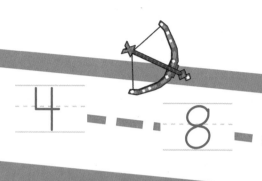

4

8

16

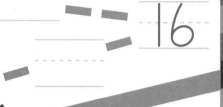

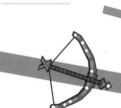

60

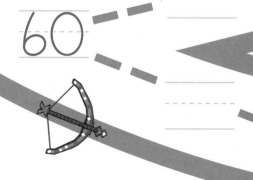

ANSWER KEY

Page 6: Addition By Grouping
2. 16
3. 31
4. 21
5. 17

Page 7: Mystery Message with Addition and Subtraction
2. 3
3. 11
4. 2
5. 13
6. 6
7. 15
8. 7
9. 14
A: Because they have bad STABLE MANNERS

Page 8: Zombie's Guide to Place Value
2. 4 tens 5 ones
3. 2 tens 5 ones
4. 3 tens 1 one
5. 2 tens 8 ones
6. 6 tens 7 ones
7. 5 tens 4 ones

Page 9: Skip Count Challenge
8, 10, 12, 14, 16, 18, 20, 22, 24

Page 10: Telling Time
2. 4:30
3. 11:00
4. 9:30
5. 7:30
6. 5:00

Page 11: Counting Money
2. 23 cents
3. 36 cents
4. 60 cents
5. 37 cents
6. 41 cents
7. 9 cents

Hardcore Mode:
8. 5 nickels

Page 12: Adventures in Geometry

1.

2.

Page 13:
3. 9

4.

5.

6. Hardcore Mode: 1/2

Page 14: Word Problems
1. 1
2. 5
3. 4

Page 15:
4. 8
5. 11
6. 6
7. 9
8. 3

Page 16: Ghast's Guide to Place Value
2. 4 tens, 3 ones
3. 3 tens, 5 ones
4. 2 tens, 9 ones
5. 4 tens, 7 ones
6. 8 tens, 9 ones
7. 6 tens, 3 ones

Page 17: Skip Count Challenge

20, 25, 30, 35, 40, 45, 50, 55, 60

Page 18: All in a Day's Work

2. G
3. F
4. C
5. A
6. B
7. D

Page 19: Time for Matching

2.

3. 4.

5. 6.

Page 20: Learning About Shapes

1. C
2. A
3. D
4. B

Page 21: Find the Shapes

5. Rectangle
6. Square
7. Circle
8.

Page 22: Addition by Grouping

2. 32
3. 26
4. 28
5. 19

Page 23: Mystery Message with Addition and Subtraction

2. 19
3. 3
4. 14
5. 17
6. 18
7. 13
8. 15
9. 11
10. 8
11. 7
12. 16

A: HE HAD NO BODY TO GO WITH

Page 24: The Enderman Number Challenge

1. D
2. E
3. B
4. A
5. C

Page 25: Skip Count Challenge

30, 40, 50, 60; 80, 90, 100, 110, 120

Page 26: The Tallest Tower

a. 7 Blocks
b. 4 Blocks
c. 6 Blocks

1. A
2. B
3. 3 Blocks

Page 27: The Tallest Tower, cont'd

Tower	Number of Blocks Tall	Color
A	7	GRAY
B	4	GRAY
C	6	GRAY
D	5	GRAY

Page 29: Adventures in Geometry

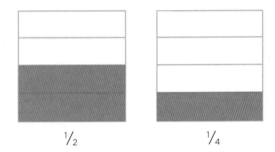

½   ¼

Page 30-31: Word Problems

2. 13 blocks of lava
3. 9 ghasts
4. 22 weapons
5. 17 cookies
6. 14 hunger points
7. 3 items
8. 16 pet cats

Page 32: Creeper's Guide to Place Value

2. Hundreds:7 Tens:6 Ones:0
3. Hundreds:5 Tens:9 Ones:2
4. Hundreds:1 Tens:8 Ones:4
5. Hundreds:5 Tens:3 Ones:2
6. Hundreds:9 Tens:5 Ones:6
7. Hundreds:4 Tens:5 Ones:3

Page 33: Skip Count Challenge

112; 114, 115, 116, 117, 118, 119, 120, 121, 122, 123

Page 34: Mobs and Monsters

	Creeper	Zombie	Ghast	Enderman	Cave Spider	Snow Golem
0 Legs	X					X
2 Legs		X		X		
More than 2 Legs			X		X	

1. 2 mobs
2. 4 mobs
3. Enderman and cave spider

Page 35: Counting Money

1. 13 cents
2. 15 cents
3. 35 cents
4. 29 cents
5. 36 cents

Hardcore Mode: 6. 128 cents, or $1.28

Page 36: Adventures in Geometry: Spot the Shapes

1. Trapezoid
2. Rectangle
3. Square

Page 38: Sandstone Addition

1. 76
2. 97
3. 75
4. 84
5. 97
6. 98
7. 97
8. 74
9. 86
10. 59
11. 36
12. 109

Hidden Message: DESERT

Page 39: Subtraction Mystery Message

1. 13
2. 44
3. 61
4. 15

5. 21
6. 71
7. 11
8. 42
9. 26
10. 53
A: POP MUSIC, OF COURSE

Page 40: Mob Monster Showdown

1. <
2. >
3. <
4. <
5. >
6. <
7. <

Enderman

Page 41: Skip Count Challenge

6; 12, 15, 18, 21, 24, 27, 30, 33, 36, 39, 42, 45

Page 42-43: Telling Time

2. 4:15
3. 6:10
4. 8:25
5. 3:50
6. 1:55
7. 12:40
8. 9:05
9. 6:45
10. 2:35
11. 1:10
12. 10:25
13. 5:55
14. 6:40

Page 44: 4 Sides are Better Than 1

1.

2.

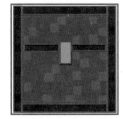

3.

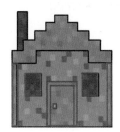

Page 46: Addition & Subtraction Mystery Number

1. 3
2. 7
3. 10
4. 8
5. 6
6. 14
7. 7
8. 3
9. 7

Page 47: Mystery Message with Addition Using Regrouping

1. 54
2. 96
3. 41
4. 40
5. 44
6. 31
7. 73
8. 93
9. 70
10. 72

A: ONE. AFTER THAT IT'S NOT EMPTY.

Page 48: Pigman's Guide to Place Value

1. 3
2. 9
3. 2
4. 8
5. 4
6. 1
7. 9

Page 49: Skip Count Challenge

12; 20, 24, 28, 32, 36, 40, 44, 48, 52, 56; 64, 68

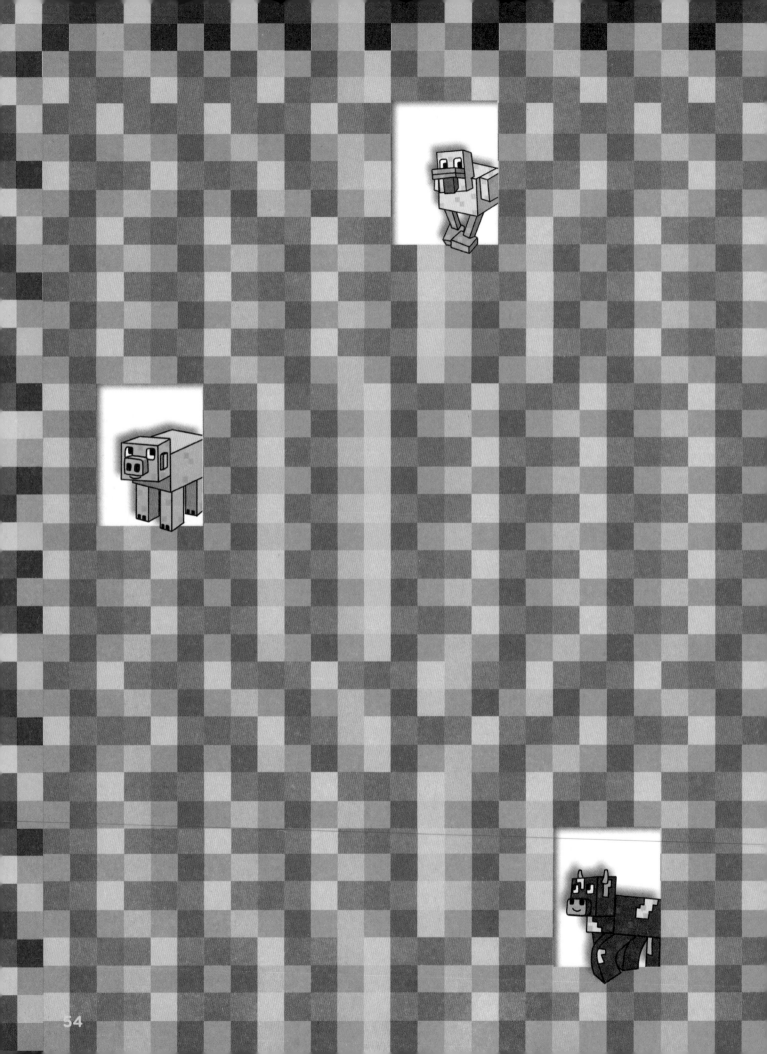

MATH FOR MINECRAFTERS

WORD PROBLEMS

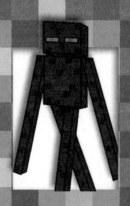

ADDING AND SUBTRACTING NUMBERS FROM 0 TO 10

Read the problem carefully. Use the pictures for extra help.
Write the answer in the space provided.

1. A skeleton shoots 7 arrows at you. Another skeleton shoots 2 arrows. How many arrows are shot at you?

2. You are attacked by 6 silverfish. You destroy 1 of them. How many silverfish are left?

3. A ghast shoots 10 fireballs at you. Only 2 of them hit you. How many fireballs miss you?

4. You spawn 10 creepers. You get out of the way as 3 of them blow up. How many creepers are left?

5. You find 7 shulkers in an End temple. You attack and destroy 4 of them. How many are left?

6. You place 3 torches on a cave wall but it's still really dark. You add 3 more torches to the wall. How many torches are on the wall?

7. You brew 4 potions of Strength and 2 potions of Night Vision. How many potions do you brew in all?

8. You start your game with 9 shovels in your inventory. You break 4 of them while digging. How many shovels do you have left?

9. You teleport 2 times in the morning and 2 times later in the day. How many times do you teleport?

10. You have 3 pieces of rotten flesh in your inventory. You attack zombies and get 4 more. How many pieces of rotten flesh do you have now?

11. You collect 8 gold ingots and use 2 of them to make a sword. How many gold ingots do you have left?

12. You find 6 chests in a cave and 4 more in another player's home. How many chests do you find in all?

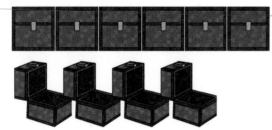

13. You mine 10 blocks of obsidian. Then you use 3 of the blocks to build a tower. How many obsidian blocks do you have left?

14. You use 5 redstone blocks to build a wall. You use 5 more blocks to make the wall longer. How many redstone blocks do you use in all?

15. A group of 4 zombies attacks you in the night. Another group of 5 zombies attacks you later that night. How many zombies attack you in all?

HARDCORE MODE

Steve, Alex, and a villager collect as many purpur blocks as possible. Steve collects only 5 purpur blocks. The villager collects 4 more than Steve. Alex finds the most. She collects 3 more than the villager. How many purpur blocks does Alex collect?

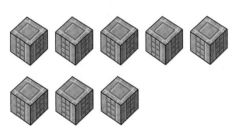

MATH RIDDLE CHALLENGE

Use your math smarts to fill in the answer to the riddle below:

Why don't zombies like running in races?

14 S   10 L   2 D   8 D   6 A   4 E   12 A   16 T

Count by **2s** to figure out the order of the letters above in the blank spaces below.

Because they always come in __ __ __ __   __ __ __ __ .

You've earned 10 math experience points!

ADDING THREE NUMBERS FROM 0 TO 10

Read the problem carefully. Use the pictures for extra help.
Write the answer in the space provided.

1.  You build 2 towers, 2 beds, and 1 cobblestone house. How many things do you build in all?

2. You ride the rail cart for 3 minutes in the morning, 4 minutes in the afternoon, and 1 minute at night. How long do you ride the rail cart?

3. 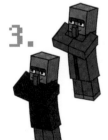 You trade 5 items with a blacksmith villager, 4 items with a priest villager, and 1 more item with a farmer villager. How many items do you trade in all?

4. You tame 1 wolf today, 2 wolves tomorrow, and 6 more wolves the next day. How many wolves do you tame in all?

ADDING THREE NUMBERS FROM 0 TO 10

(continued from previous page)

5. You fence in a group of 3 sheep. You bring 2 more sheep inside the fence. While the gate is open, 2 more sheep wander inside. How many sheep are fenced in now?

6. You get 5 experience points from every creeper you kill. You kill 2 creepers. How many experience points do you get?

7. You mine 7 blocks of redstone, 2 blocks of obsidian, and 1 block of granite. How many blocks do you mine in all?

8. You destroy 3 Endermen, 1 creeper, and 3 zombie pigmen. How many hostile mobs do you destroy?

9. A witch throws 6 potions of Poison, 3 potions of Slowness and 1 potion of Weakness. How many potions does the witch throw?

10. 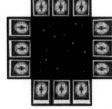 You see 5 Endermen when you enter the End, 2 as you are fighting the Ender Dragon, and 1 more before you escape through the portal. How many Endermen do you see?

11. You tame 5 ocelots in the morning, 2 in the afternoon, and 2 more the next day. How many ocelots do you tame?

12. You discover 3 biomes in the Overworld, 1 in the Nether, and 1 in the End. How many biomes do you discover in all?

ADDING THREE NUMBERS FROM 0 TO 10

(continued from previous page)

13. You trade 3 emeralds to one villager and 3 more emeralds to the next villager you meet. You trade 1 more emerald to a third villager. How many emeralds do you trade in all?

14. You craft 2 iron chest plates, 3 iron helmets, and 1 shield. How many pieces of armor do you craft in all?

15. A skeleton shoots 7 arrows at you, 1 at a villager, and 2 at an iron golem. How many arrows does he shoot in all?

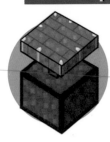

HARDCORE MODE

There are 4 desert temples. Each one has 2 active traps. You deactivate 1 trap by breaking the pressure plate. How many active traps are left?

MATH RIDDLE CHALLENGE

Use your math smarts to fill in the answer to the riddle below:

What material do Minecrafters use to build their libraries?

32 N   8 E   16 D   28 O   4 R   24 T   12 A   20 S

Count by **4s** to figure out the order of the letters above in the blank spaces below.

__ __ __ __ - __ __ __ __ e **of course!**

You've earned 10 math experience points!

SUBTRACTING THREE NUMBERS FROM 0 TO 10

Read the problem carefully. Use the pictures for extra help. Write the answer in the space provided.

1. You catch 10 fish with your fishing rod. You feed 3 to your cat and eat 2. How many fish are left?

2. There are 7 bats in a dungeon. You scare 2 away and destroy 1. How many bats are left?

3.  There are 6 villagers. During the night, 2 get turned into zombie villagers and wander away. One villager falls off a ledge. How many villagers are left?

4. You have 8 diamond swords. You place 6 swords in a chest that gets blown up. You break 2 swords after using them for hours on end. How many diamond swords are left?

5. You get 10 skeleton spawn eggs in Creative mode. When used, 4 of them turn into wither skeletons and 1 burns up in the daylight. How many are left?

6. You find a wall made of 9 blocks of sandstone. You break 3 blocks with a wooden pickaxe, stop to rest, and then break 4 more blocks with a shovel. How many blocks of sandstone are left?

7. You have 7 diamonds. You use 3 to make diamond leggings and 2 to make a diamond sword. How many diamonds do you have left?

8. You have 8 blocks of wool in three colors: pink, lime, and yellow. 2 blocks are pink and 2 are yellow. How many blocks of lime wool do you have?

SUBTRACTING THREE NUMBERS FROM 0 TO 10

(continued from previous page)

9. You approach a monster spawner in an Overworld dungeon. It spawns 6 monsters, including 2 spiders, 1 zombie, and some skeletons. How many skeletons are spawned?

10. You have 9 items in your inventory. 3 of them are food items, 2 are weapons, and the rest are building materials. How many items in your inventory are building materials?

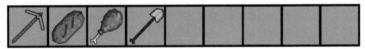

11. You battle the Ender Dragon a total of 10 times. You get destroyed by the Ender Dragon once and destroyed by Endermen twice. The rest of the times you win. How many times do you win?

12. You battle 7 zombies near a lava pit. You use a Knockback enchantment to send 4 zombies flying backward into a lava pit. Then 2 zombies burn up in the daylight. How many zombies are left?

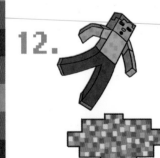

13. You start your game with 8 bones. You use 3 bones to make bone meal and 3 more to tame wolves. How many bones do you have left?

14. You battle 8 ghasts in the Nether. One ghast is destroyed when you deflect its fireballs and 3 more are destroyed by your arrows. How many ghasts are left?

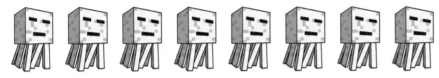

15. You start your game with 10 hearts. You fall off a hill and lose 3 hearts. You get hit by a zombie and lose 1 heart. How many hearts do you have left?

HARDCORE MODE

You craft 10 tools and 6 of them are shovels. The rest are equally divided between swords and pickaxes. How many swords and pickaxes did you craft?

Use your math smarts to fill in the answer to the riddle below:

What did Alex say as she prepared to battle the skeleton horse?

30 T   10 B   40 I   5 A   25 E   15 O   45 C   35 P   20 N

Count by **5s** to figure out the order of the letters above in the blank spaces below.

I've got __   __ __ __ __   __ o __ __ __ k
with you .

You've earned 10 math experience points!

ADDING NUMBERS FROM 0 TO 20

Read the problem carefully. Use the pictures for extra help.
Write the answer in the space provided.

1. You are collecting Eyes of Ender to build an End portal. You get 6 Eyes of Ender from villagers and you craft 7 more. How many Eyes of Ender do you have in all?

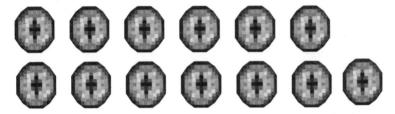

2. You make 10 bowls of mushroom stew and each bowl restores 2 hunger points. How many hunger points do you restore if you eat all of the mushroom stew?

3. You destroy a pair of snow golems. The first snow golem drops 8 snowballs, and the second snow golem drops 6. How many snowballs are dropped in all?

4. You craft 9 boats one week and 9 more boats the next week. How many boats do you craft in all?

5. There are 9 regular apples in your inventory and 7 golden apples. How many apples are in your inventory?

6. You catch 4 pufferfish to make potion of Water Breathing. You catch 8 more pufferfish. How many pufferfish do you catch in all?

7. A polar bear drops 6 fish. Another polar bear drops 6 more fish. How many fish are dropped in all?

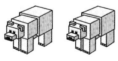

8. You craft 5 Jack o'Lanterns in the morning and 7 Jack o'Lanterns later in the day. How many Jack o'Lanterns do you craft in all?

9. Your farm has 7 cows and 6 chickens. How many animals does your farm have in all?

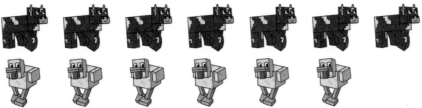

10. 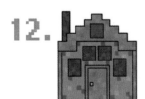 You keep 7 pieces of armor in one chest and 8 pieces of armor in another. How many pieces of armor do you keep in all?

11. It takes you 14 minutes to craft a house and 6 minutes to craft a bed. How many minutes do you spend crafting both?

12. Your cobblestone house has 5 windows in the front and 6 windows in the back. How many windows does it have in all?

13. You fight 6 Wither skeletons and 9 blazes in the Nether fortress. How many hostile mobs do you fight in all?

14. You place 8 grass blocks in a row. You place 8 more behind them. How many grass blocks do you place?

15.  You use your enchantment table to enchant 5 diamond swords and 6 iron shovels. How many items do you enchant in all?

HARDCORE MODE

If you encounter 6 wither skeletons and 3 blazes every time you enter the Nether fortress and you enter the Nether fortress 4 times, how many wither skeletons do you encounter in all?

MATH RIDDLE CHALLENGE

Use your math smarts to fill in the answer to the riddle below:

Why is it so easy to get around in the Overworld?

18 L 36 K 42 W 24 O 12 B 30 C 48 Y 6 A

Count by **6s** to figure out the order of the letters above in the blank spaces below.

Because everything there is just __   __ __ __ __ __

a __ a __ .

You've earned 10 math experience points!

SUBTRACTING NUMBERS FROM 0 TO 20

Read the problem carefully. Use the pictures for extra help. Write the answer in the space provided.

1. You start a game with 14 hunger points and lose 7 hunger points after a long day of digging. How many hunger points do you have left?

2. You swing your sword at a zombie 12 times, but you make contact only 4 of those times. How many times do you swing your sword and miss?

3. You battle 13 creepers in the Overworld. Your tamed wolf destroys 8 of them. How many are left for you to destroy?

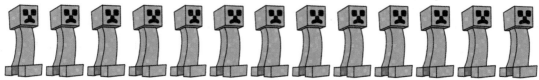

4. Squids drop 20 ink sacs into the water, but you are only able to collect 6 before you come up for air. How many ink sacs are still in the water?

5.  You have 17 minutes until nightfall and you spend 3 of those minutes crafting a bed. How many minutes are left until nightfall?

6. You have 13 empty buckets. You fill 6 of them with milk. How many empty buckets are left?

7. You meet 20 ocelots in the Jungle Biome. You tame 4 of them and they follow you home. How many ocelots are left untamed?

8. You have 17 blocks, but you only need 9 blocks to build a beacon. How many blocks do you have left over after you build your beacon?

9. You are attacked by 12 spiders, but you kill 5 of them. How many spiders are left?

10. Creepers drop 14 units of gunpowder. You collect 9 of them. How many units of gunpowder are left?

11. You find 16 cobwebs in an abandoned mineshaft. You use your shears to collect 3 of them. How many cobwebs are left?

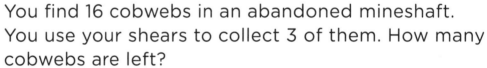

12. Zombie pigmen attack a village where 19 villagers live. When you arrive at the village, only 4 villagers have survived. How many villagers were destroyed in the attack?

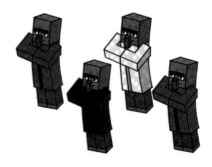

13. A ghast hurls 11 fireballs at you. You are hit by 5 of them. How many fireballs miss you?

14. You have 16 spawn eggs in your inventory. You use 3 of them. How many spawn eggs do you have left?

15. You are trying to build an 18-step staircase out of wood blocks. You build 9 steps and stop to eat. How many more steps do you need to build?

HARDCORE MODE

If each of the Wither's 3 heads spits 8 skulls at you during a battle and 14 out of all the skulls miss you, how many skulls hit you?

Use your math smarts to fill in the answer to the riddle below:

Why does Steve hate driving places?

28 D   35 B   14 R   56 K   7 A   42 L   21 O   49 C

Count by **7s** to figure out the order of the letters above in the blank spaces below.

Because he's always hitting

__ __ __ a __   __ __ o __ __

You've earned 10 math experience points!

ADDING AND SUBTRACTING NUMBERS FROM 0 TO 20

Read the problem carefully. Use the pictures for extra help.
Write the answer in the space provided.

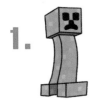

1.  You put down 14 minecart rails and a creeper blows up 6 of them. How many rails are left?

2. You transport 15 chests to your base using your new railway system. You transport 5 more. How many chests do you transport in all?

3. You visit the Desert Biome 12 times and the Jungle Biome 7 times. How many more times do you visit the Desert Biome?

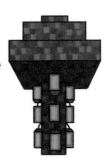

4. A group of 15 zombie villagers are headed your way. You only have enough splash potion and golden apples to turn 7 of them back into villagers. How many will remain zombies?

ADDING AND SUBTRACTING NUMBERS FROM 0 TO 20

(continued from previous page)

5. You ride 6 pigs and 12 horses with your new leather saddle. How many animals do you ride in all?

6.  You come across a herd of 16 mooshrooms grazing in the Mushroom Island Biome. You count 8 baby mooshrooms, but the rest are adults. How many adult mooshrooms are in the herd?

7. You drink 4 potions of Swiftness and 9 potions of Strength. How many potions do you drink in all?

8. You visit the End 11 times, but find Elytra only 4 of those times. How many times do you visit the End and not find Elytra?

9. An iron golem drops 13 red flowers. You collect 6 of them. How many flowers are left?

10. You want to mine 17 layers of diamond ore. You mine 4 layers. How many layers are left to mine?

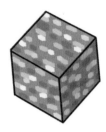

11. You dig through 12 layers of lapis lazuli ore and rest. You dig through 6 more. How many layers of lapis lazuli ore do you dig through?

12. You need 20 iron blocks to build a small shelter. You only have 3 of them. How many more blocks do you need?

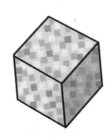

ADDING AND SUBTRACTING NUMBERS FROM 0 TO 20

(continued from previous page)

13.  You need 11 ingredients to make a potion. You only have 4 of the ingredients. How many more ingredients do you need?

14. You chop down a total of 13 trees. You eat to restore your hunger points and then chop down 5 more. How many trees do you chop in all?

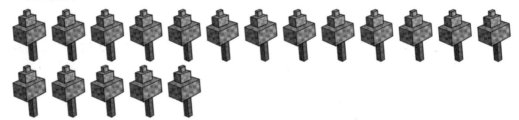

15. You climb 11 steps of stairs on your way to collect some diamonds. You climb 7 more steps. How many steps do you climb in all?

HARDCORE MODE

It takes 6 bites for a player to finish eating a cake. How many bites does it take for a player to eat 3 and a half cakes?

MATH RIDDLE CHALLENGE

Use your math smarts to fill in the answer to the riddle below:

What does Steve tell himself before he steps bravely through the portal?

 40 E 16 N 8 I 32 H 64 D 24 T 48 E 56 N

Count by **8s** to figure out the order of the letters above in the blank spaces below.

"It will all work out __ __   __ __ __   __ __ __."

You've earned 10 math experience points!

ADDING THREE NUMBERS FROM 0 TO 20

Read the problem carefully. Use the pictures for extra help.
Write the answer in the space provided.

1. You craft 1 brewing stand, 15 pressure plates, and 4 firework rockets. How many items do you craft in all?

2. You destroy 5 hostile mobs, 6 neutral mobs, and 2 boss mobs. How many mobs do you destroy?

3. You build a tower with 7 clay blocks, 4 granite blocks, and 6 gravel blocks. How many blocks do you use to build your tower?

4. While you're playing, 3 herds of cows spawn. One herd has 7 cows, another herd has 5 cows, and the last herd has 6 cows. How many cows spawn in all?

5. Zombies spawn in groups of 4. While you're playing, 3 groups of zombies spawn in the Overworld. How many zombies spawn in all?

6. You trade 12 emeralds to the first villager you see, 2 emeralds to the next villager, and 3 more to the next villager. How many emeralds do you trade in all?

7.  You build 9 beacons your first day, 2 beacons the next day, and 3 beacons the third day. How many beacons do you build in all?

8. You place 5 minecart rails in the morning, 7 in the afternoon, and 7 more later that night. How many minecart rails do you place in all?

ADDING THREE NUMBERS FROM 0 TO 20

(continued from previous page)

9. You battle 9 skeletons, 4 zombies, and 3 creepers in one day of gaming. How many mobs do you battle in all?

10. You enchant 3 books, 8 swords, and 2 pieces of armor. How many items do you enchant in all?

11. You shoot 7 arrows at a creeper, 8 at a skeleton, and 4 at a giant zombie. How many arrows do you shoot in all?

12. You survive 2 creeper explosions at your spawn point, 5 more near your farm, and 5 more inside your shelter. How many creeper explosions do you survive?

13.  A witch throws 1 potion of Slowness, 3 potions of Weakness, and 8 potions of Poison. How many potions does the witch throw in all?

14. You tame 6 wolves, 3 horses, and 7 ocelots. How many animals do you tame in all?

15. The Ender Dragon fires 6 Ender charges at you when it first circles you, 6 more as it circles the second time, and 7 more before you succeed in defeating it. How many Ender charges does the Ender Dragon fire in all?

HARDCORE MODE

You battle 8 ghasts and take a little damage. You battle two more pairs of ghasts and take more damage. How many ghasts do you battle in all?

MATH RIDDLE CHALLENGE

Use your math smarts to fill in the answer to the riddle below:

Why doesn't anyone want to play with the Ender Dragon or the Wither?

 45 O 9 T 63 S 18 O 72 Y 54 S 36 B 27 O

Count by **9s** to figure out the order of the letters above in the blank spaces below.

Because they're __ __ __   __ __ __ __- __!

You've earned 10 math experience points!

SUBTRACTION WITH THREE NUMBERS FROM 0 TO 20

Read the problem carefully. Use the pictures for extra help.
Write the answer in the space provided.

1. You start with 18 experience points, but you use 4 of those points enchanting a bow and arrow and 1 point enchanting a book. How many experience points do you have left?

2. You place 14 lily pads on water blocks to cross a river, but 6 of them are destroyed by a boat and 3 more are caught by a fisherman villager. How many lily pads are left?

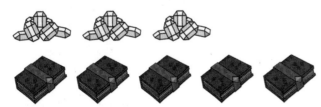

3. A stack of three cacti is 19 blocks tall. One cactus is 5 blocks tall and another cactus is 4 blocks tall. How many blocks tall is the third cactus?

4. You place 15 items in your chest. You know that 3 of them are diamonds and 5 of them are enchanted books. The rest are gunpowder. How many items of gunpowder do you have in your chest?

SUBTRACTION WITH THREE NUMBERS FROM 0 TO 20

(continued from previous page)

5. You meet 15 villagers in one day. Of those villagers, 4 are blacksmith villagers and 1 is a priest villager. The rest of the villagers are librarians. How many of the villagers are librarians?

6. There are 12 snow golems. Of those snow golems, 2 melt in a sudden rainstorm and 3 melt in the Jungle Biome. How many snow golems are left?

7.  You chop down 13 trees. Six of them are oak trees, 3 of them are birch trees, and the rest are spruce trees. How many trees are spruce trees?

8. You collect 20 Ender pearls after battling a group of Endermen. You use 4 of those Ender pearls to make an Eye of Ender. You lose 2 of them when a mob steals your treasure chest. How many Ender pearls do you still have?

9.  You have 17 lumps of coal in your inventory. You burn 12 in your furnace and trade 4 to villagers. How many lumps of coal do you have left?

10.  You have 11 zombie eggs in your inventory. You spawn zombies from 5 of the eggs and baby zombies from 3 of the eggs. The rest of the eggs are still in your inventory. How many zombie eggs are still in your inventory?

11. You are down to 0 hunger points. You get 14 hunger points from eating cookies. You lose 5 hunger points while battling, and lose 5 more hunger points while mining. How many hunger points do you have left?

12. You brew 13 potions of Weakness. You use 6 potions (plus some golden apples) to heal zombie villagers and 2 to weaken skeletons during a battle. How many potions of Weakness do you have left?

13. Your first full day of Minecrafting lasts for 20 minutes. You spend 9 minutes searching for resources and 3 minutes building structures. How many minutes do you have until the day ends?

14. You have 19 wood planks. You use 4 to make a boat and 3 to make a bed. How many wood planks do you have left?

15. You see 14 donkeys in the Plains Biome. In the next few minutes, 6 of them wander away and 2 are blown up by a creeper. How many donkeys are left?

HARDCORE MODE

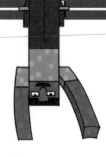

Your mom gives you 30 minutes of gaming time. You spend up 8 of those minutes trying to remember your password, so you ask your mom for more gaming time. Your mom lets you add 4 minutes to your gaming time. How much gaming time do you have now?

MATH RIDDLE CHALLENGE

Use your math smarts to fill in the answer to the riddle below:

What does an Enderman pack when he goes on vacation?

90 A 30 A 10 C 80 E 60 E 40 E 100 R 20 N 50 N 70 R

Count by **10s** to figure out the order of the letters above in the blank spaces below.

He packs lots of __ l __ __ n __ __d__ __- w __ __ __!

You've earned 10 math experience points!

ADDING AND SUBTRACTING THREE OR FOUR NUMBERS FROM 0 TO 20

Read the problem carefully. Use the pictures for extra help. Write the answer in the space provided.

1. You are attacked by a group of 16 Endermen. You destroy 2 of them with your sword. You scare 6 Endermen away with water. How many Endermen are still attacking?

2. You battle a group of 5 ghasts in the Nether. Each ghast shoots 2 fireballs at you. You deflect 3 of the fireballs, but the rest of the them hit you and destroy you. How many fireballs hit you?

3. You build 5 cobblestone structures, 7 wood structures, and 4 obsidian structures. How many structures do you build in all?

4. You want to cure 12 zombie villagers, but you only have enough golden apples to cure 4 of them. You craft a few more golden apples and cure 3 more zombie villagers. How many villagers are still zombies?

5. A group of 20 zombies approach a village. An iron golem attacks and destroys 6 of the zombies. You destroy 3 of the zombies. How many zombies are left?

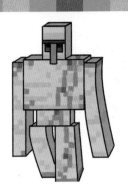

6. 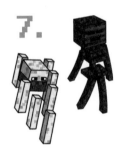 You craft 11 iron swords, 4 golden swords, and 3 chest plates. After many battles, 6 of the iron swords break. How many swords are left?

7. 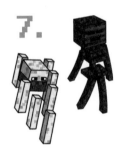 You craft a brewing stand and use it to brew 14 potions. You use 5 potions on a blaze, 1 on a wither skeleton, and 2 on zombie pigmen. How many potions are left?

8. You craft 17 items. Of those, 5 are swords. The rest are an equal amount of chest plates and helmets. How many chest plates and helmets do you craft?

ADDING AND SUBTRACTING THREE OR FOUR NUMBERS FROM 0 TO 20

(continued from previous page)

9. There are 14 hostile mobs that walk into lava blocks. If 6 of the hostile mobs are zombie pigmen (which are immune to fire), 3 are ghasts (also immune to fire), and the rest take damage, how many hostile mobs take damage?

10. You collect 9 gold ingots one day, 5 the next, and 10 the next. You use 4 of them to make a clock. How many gold ingots do you have left?

11. You make 6 wooden hoes one day and 3 the next. It takes 2 wooden sticks to make a wooden hoe. How many sticks did you use to make all of the wooden hoes?

12. You face the Wither 17 times in one week. You escape 3 times and are destroyed 12 times. The rest of the times, you defeat the Wither. How many times do you defeat the Wither?

13. You need 20 diamonds to make full diamond armor. You mine 7 from diamond ore and you collect 4 more from a chest. How many more diamonds do you need to make full armor?

14. You teleport 8 times in the morning and 7 times in the afternoon. If you teleport 18 times total that day, how many more times do you teleport?

15. You catch 4 fish in the morning, 16 fish later that day, and 2 more in the evening. You use 7 of your fish to tame ocelots. How many fish are left?

HARDCORE MODE

Write your own addition or subtraction problem below and show it to your friend, your teacher, or your parent. Challenge them to solve it!

_____

_____

_____

MATH RIDDLE CHALLENGE

Use your math smarts to fill in the answer to the riddle below:

Why did Steve place a chicken on top of a shining tower?

 110 S   88 G   55 O   44 C   11 B   33 A   77 E   66 N   22 E   99 G

Count by **11s** to figure out the order of the letters above in the blank spaces below.

He wanted to make _ _ _ _ _ _ and _ _ _ _!

You've earned 10 math experience points!

ADDING NUMBERS FROM 0 TO 100

Read the problem carefully. Use the pictures for extra help. Write the answer in the space provided.

1. You spawn 26 husks in the desert biome and 13 baby husks. How many husks do you spawn in all?

2. You stack 24 blocks of glowstone on top of 33 blocks of gold ore. How many blocks are stacked in all?

3. You see 18 spiders while exploring a cave and 11 more on your way back to your shelter. How many spiders do you see in all?

4. You catch 14 pufferfish on your first day fishing and 67 regular fish the second day. How many fish do you catch in all?

5.  You are attacked by 22 slimes one night and 37 slimes another night. How many slimes attack you in all?

6. 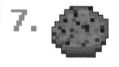 You and your tamed wolf battle a group of endermites. Your wolf destroys 15 and you destroy 63. How many endermites do you destroy in all?

7. You eat 45 cookies to gain hunger points. You eat 12 mushroom stew to gain more hunger points. How many food items do you eat in all?

8.  In the course of a day, you battle a lot of witches. They drop 13 spider eyes and 22 glass bottles. How many items do the witches drop in all?

CONGRATULATIONS

YOU'VE EARNED

THE POTION OF MATH ABILITY!

This potion gives you the ability to tackle math challenges of all kinds.

Count up your experience points from the Math Riddle Challenge pages and write the total below:

ANSWER KEY

PAGE 56

1. 9 arrows
2. 5 silverfish
3. 8 fireballs
4. 7 creepers

PAGE 57

5. 3 shulkers
6. 6 torches
7. 6 potions
8. 5 shovels

PAGE 58

9. 4 times
10. 7 pieces
11. 6 gold ingots
12. 10 chests

PAGE 59

13. 7 obsidian blocks
14. 10 redstone blocks
15. 9 zombies

Hardcore mode

12 purpur blocks

PAGE 60

Mystery Message 1

Why don't zombies like running in races?
Because they always come in dead last.

PAGE 61

1. 5 things
2. 8 minutes
3. 10 items
4. 9 wolves

PAGE 62

5. 7 sheep
6. 10 experience points
7. 10 blocks
8. 7 hostile mobs

PAGE 63

9. 10 potions
10. 8 Endermen
11. 9 ocelots
12. 5 biomes

PAGE 64

13. 7 emeralds
14. 6 pieces of armor
15. 10 arrows

Hardcore mode

7 traps

PAGE 65

What material do Minecrafters' use to build their libraries?
Answer: read-stone

PAGE 66

1. 5 fish
2. 4 bats
3. 3 villagers
4. 0 diamond swords

PAGE 67

5. 5 skeleton spawn eggs
6. 2 blocks of sandstone
7. 2 diamonds
8. 4 blocks of lime

PAGE 68

9. 3 skeletons
10. 4 building materials
11. 7 times
12. 1 zombie

PAGE 69

13. 2 bones
14. 4 ghasts
15. 6 hearts

Hardcore mode

2 swords, 2 pickaxes

PAGE 70

What did Alex say as she prepared to battle the skeleton horse?

I've got a bone to pick with you!

PAGE 71

1. 13 Eyes of Ender
2. 20 hunger points
3. 14 snowballs
4. 18 boats

PAGE 72

5. 16 apples
6. 12 pufferfish
7. 12 fish
8. 12 Jack o'Lanterns

PAGE 73

9. 13 animals
10. 15 pieces of armor
11. 20 minutes
12. 11 windows

PAGE 74

13. 15 hostile mobs
14. 16 grass blocks
15. 11 items

Hardcore mode

24 wither skeletons

PAGE 75

Why is it so easy to get around in the Overworld?

Because everything there is just a block away.

PAGE 76

1. 7 hunger points
2. 8 swings
3. 5 creepers
4. 14 ink sacs

PAGE 77

5. 14 minutes
6. 7 buckets
7. 16 ocelots
8. 8 blocks

PAGE 78

9. 7 spiders
10. 5 units
11. 13 cobwebs
12. 15 villagers

PAGE 79

13. 6 fireballs
14. 13 spawn eggs
15. 9 more steps

Hardcore mode

10 skulls

PAGE 80

Why does Steve hate driving places?

Because he's always hitting a road block.

PAGE 81

1. 8 rails
2. 20 chests
3. 5 more times
4. 8 villagers

PAGE 82

5. 18 animals
6. 8 adult mooshrooms
7. 13 potions
8. 7 times

PAGE 83

9. 7 flowers
10. 13 layers
11. 18 layers
12. 17 blocks

PAGE 84

13. 7 ingredients
14. 18 trees
15. 18 steps

Hardcore mode

21 bites

PAGE 85

What does Steve tell himself before he steps bravely through the portal?

"It will all work out in the End."

PAGE 86

1. 20 items
2. 13 mobs
3. 17 blocks
4. 18 cows

PAGE 87

5. 12 zombies
6. 17 emeralds
7. 14 beacons
8. 19 minecart rails

PAGE 88

9. 16 mobs
10. 13 items
11. 19 arrows
12. 12 explosions

PAGE 89

13. 12 potions
14. 16 animals
15. 19 Ender charges

Hardcore mode

12 ghasts

PAGE 90

Why doesn't anyone want to play with the Ender Dragon or the Wither?

Because they're too boss-y. (Get it? They're boss mobs!)

PAGE 91

1. 13 experience points
2. 5 lily pads
3. 10 blocks
4. 7 items of gunpowder

PAGE 92

5. 10 villagers
6. 7 snow golems
7. 4 spruce trees
8. 14 Ender pearls

PAGE 93

9. 1 lump of coal
10. 3 zombie eggs
11. 4 hunger points
12. 5 potions of Weakness

PAGE 94

13. 8 minutes
14. 12 wood planks
15. 6 donkeys

Hardcore mode

26 minutes of gaming time

PAGE 95

What does an Enderman pack when he goes on vacation?

He packs lots of clean Enderwear!

PAGE 96

1. 8 Endermen
2. 7 fireballs
3. 16 structures
4. 5 villagers

PAGE 97

5. 11 zombies
6. 9 swords
7. 6 potions
8. 6 chest plates and 6 helmets

PAGE 98

9. 5 mobs
10. 20 gold ingots
11. 18 sticks
12. 2 times

PAGE 99

13. 9 diamonds
14. 3 times
15. 15 fish

PAGE 100

Why did Steve place a chicken on top of a shining tower?

He wanted to make beacon and eggs!

PAGE 101

1. 39 husks
2. 57 blocks
3. 29 spiders
4. 81 fish

PAGE 102

5. 59 slimes
6. 78 endermites
7. 57 food items
8. 35 items

MATH FOR MINECRAFTERS

MATH FACTS

MATH FACTS PROGRESS TRACKER

Date	Page Number or Skill Practiced	# Correct in One Minute

ADDITION MATH FACTS FROM 0 TO 10

1. $\begin{array}{r} 3 \\ +\ 4 \\ \hline \end{array}$
2. $\begin{array}{r} 3 \\ +\ 3 \\ \hline \end{array}$
3. $\begin{array}{r} 4 \\ +\ 5 \\ \hline \end{array}$
4. $\begin{array}{r} 6 \\ +\ 2 \\ \hline \end{array}$
5. $\begin{array}{r} 6 \\ +\ 4 \\ \hline \end{array}$

6. $\begin{array}{r} 5 \\ +\ 5 \\ \hline \end{array}$
7. $\begin{array}{r} 3 \\ +\ 7 \\ \hline \end{array}$
8. $\begin{array}{r} 1 \\ +\ 5 \\ \hline \end{array}$
9. $\begin{array}{r} 5 \\ +\ 3 \\ \hline \end{array}$
10. $\begin{array}{r} 3 \\ +\ 2 \\ \hline \end{array}$

11. $\begin{array}{r} 4 \\ +\ 4 \\ \hline \end{array}$
12. $\begin{array}{r} 8 \\ +\ 1 \\ \hline \end{array}$
13. $\begin{array}{r} 4 \\ +\ 2 \\ \hline \end{array}$
14. $\begin{array}{r} 7 \\ +\ 2 \\ \hline \end{array}$
15. $\begin{array}{r} 6 \\ +\ 3 \\ \hline \end{array}$

16. $\begin{array}{r} 4 \\ +\ 3 \\ \hline \end{array}$
17. $\begin{array}{r} 8 \\ +\ 2 \\ \hline \end{array}$
18. $\begin{array}{r} 3 \\ +\ 5 \\ \hline \end{array}$
19. $\begin{array}{r} 1 \\ +\ 4 \\ \hline \end{array}$
20. $\begin{array}{r} 2 \\ +\ 5 \\ \hline \end{array}$

ADDITION MATH FACTS FROM 0 TO 10

1. 5
    + 5

2. 5
    + 2

3. 5
    + 3

4. 2
    + 6

5. 8
    + 2

6. 5
    + 4

7. 3
    + 7

8. 2
    + 3

9. 2
    + 4

10. 3
    + 4

11. 4
    + 4

12. 7
    + 2

13. 4
    + 5

14. 6
    + 2

15. 6
    + 3

16. 4
    + 3

17. 1
    + 8

18. 3
    + 5

19. 2
    + 5

20. 2
    + 2

SUBTRACTION MATH FACTS FROM 0 TO 10

1. 4
  − 2

2. 5
  − 3

3. 5
  − 2

4. 7
  − 3

5. 6
  − 3

6. 10
  − 4

7. 8
  − 4

8. 10
  − 3

9. 7
  − 4

10. 9
  − 4

11. 9
  − 2

12. 10
  − 5

13. 3
  − 1

14. 8
  − 3

15. 6
  − 2

16. 7
  − 5

17. 8
  − 2

18. 10
  − 7

19. 6
  − 1

20. 6
  − 4

SUBTRACTION MATH FACTS FROM 0 TO 10

1. 10
    − 2

2. 7
    − 3

3. 10
    − 6

4. 6
    − 3

5. 6
    − 6

6. 10
    − 4

7. 8
    − 4

8. 10
    − 3

9. 7
    − 4

10. 5
     − 4

11. 9
     − 4

12. 10
     − 5

13. 3
     − 1

14. 8
     − 3

15. 6
     − 2

16. 7
     − 5

17. 9
     − 2

18. 10
     − 7

19. 6
     − 1

20. 6
     − 4

SUBTRACTION MATH FACTS FROM 0 TO 10

1. 10
  − 4

2. 7
  − 4

3. 8
  − 3

4. 6
  − 3

5. 6
  − 5

6. 9
  − 1

7. 9
  − 5

8. 7
  − 5

9. 10
  − 3

10. 10
  − 7

11. 9
  − 6

12. 9
  − 1

13. 5
  − 1

14. 6
  − 4

15. 8
  − 4

16. 7
  − 3

17. 8
  − 2

18. 10
  − 2

19. 10
  − 6

20. 9
  − 4

SUBTRACTION MATH FACTS FROM 0 TO 10

1. 10
    − 8

2. 7
    − 5

3. 8
    − 5

4. 6
    − 3

5. 6
    − 5

6. 10
    − 6

7. 8
    − 6

8. 8
    − 3

9. 7
    − 2

10. 10
    − 7

11. 9
    − 6

12. 7
    − 3

13. 9
    − 1

14. 9
    − 4

15. 8
    − 4

16. 7
    − 4

17. 8
    − 2

18. 10
    − 4

19. 10
    − 2

20. 6
    − 4

SUBTRACTION MATH FACTS FROM 0 TO 10

1. 9
   − 8

2. 8
   − 6

3. 7
   − 5

4. 8
   − 3

5. 8
   − 8

6. 9
   − 7

7. 8
   − 4

8. 9
   − 5

9. 6
   − 6

10. 7
    − 6

11. 7
    − 7

12. 8
    − 7

13. 9
    − 9

14. 10
    − 8

15. 9
    − 6

16. 8
    − 5

17. 8
    − 8

18. 10
    − 5

19. 6
    − 3

20. 4
    − 2

ADDITION MATH FACTS FROM 0 TO 20

1. 9
    + 7

2. 8
    + 8

3. 9
    + 10

4. 4
    + 8

5. 9
    + 6

6. 6
    + 7

7. 8
    + 7

8. 9
    + 9

9. 4
    + 9

10. 7
     + 7

11. 5
     + 9

12. 6
     + 8

13. 7
     + 5

14. 8
     + 3

15. 6
     + 6

16. 4
     + 7

17. 8
     + 5

18. 7
     + 8

19. 5
     + 6

20. 7
     + 6

ADDITION MATH FACTS FROM 0 TO 20

1. 9
   + 2

2. 8
   + 3

3. 7
   + 4

4. 6
   + 5

5. 5
   + 7

6. 6
   + 7

7. 8
   + 7

8. 9
   + 9

9. 4
   + 9

10. 7
    + 7

11. 5
    + 9

12. 6
    + 8

13. 7
    + 5

14. 8
    + 4

15. 6
    + 6

16. 4
    + 7

17. 8
    + 5

18. 4
    + 8

19. 5
    + 6

20. 7
    + 6

ADDITION MATH FACTS FROM 0 TO 20

1. 9
   + 6

2. 8
   + 3

3. 7
   + 4

4. 6
   + 5

5. 7
   + 7

6. 6
   + 7

7. 8
   + 7

8. 9
   + 9

9. 4
   + 9

10. 5
    + 7

11. 5
    + 9

12. 6
    + 8

13. 7
    + 5

14. 8
    + 4

15. 3
    + 9

16. 2
    + 9

17. 8
    + 5

18. 4
    + 8

19. 8
    + 6

20. 6
    + 6

ADDITION MATH FACTS FROM 0 TO 20

1. 3
   + 8

2. 2
   + 9

3. 4
   + 7

4. 5
   + 7

5. 6
   + 6

6. 8
   + 6

7. 8
   + 5

8. 7
   + 8

9. 9
   + 9

10. 4
    + 8

11. 5
    + 9

12. 6
    + 8

13. 7
    + 9

14. 8
    + 4

15. 9
    + 3

16. 8
    + 7

17. 8
    + 8

18. 4
    + 9

19. 8
    + 3

20. 5
    + 6

ADDITION MATH FACTS FROM 0 TO 20

1. 7
   + 5
   ___

2. 7
   + 9
   ___

3. 8
   + 7
   ___

4. 9
   + 7
   ___

5. 9
   + 9
   ___

6. 6
   + 6
   ___

7. 8
   + 6
   ___

8. 4
   + 7
   ___

9. 9
   + 3
   ___

10. 4
    + 8
    ___

11. 5
    + 6
    ___

12. 6
    + 7
    ___

13. 8
    + 8
    ___

14. 8
    + 4
    ___

15. 8
    + 3
    ___

16. 9
    + 4
    ___

17. 7
    + 8
    ___

18. 3
    + 9
    ___

19. 3
    + 8
    ___

20. 5
    + 8
    ___

ADDITION MATH FACTS FROM 0 TO 20

1. 8
   + 5

2. 3
   + 9

3. 8
   + 8

4. 9
   + 8

5. 7
   + 6

6. 8
   + 6

7. 6
   + 6

8. 8
   + 7

9. 7
   + 5

10. 4
    + 8

11. 5
    + 6

12. 4
    + 7

13. 3
    + 8

14. 7
    + 4

15. 9
    + 3

16. 9
    + 9

17. 10
    + 6

18. 7
    + 9

19. 12
    + 8

20. 5
    + 8

ADDITION MATH FACTS FROM 0 TO 20

1. 7
    + 7

2. 9
    + 7

3. 10
    + 8

4. 11
    + 7

5. 12
    + 3

6. 13
    + 5

7. 14
    + 2

8. 16
    + 2

9. 2
    +10

10. 7
    +11

11. 4
    +13

12. 2
    +16

13. 1
    +17

14. 8
    + 7

15. 10
    + 3

16. 11
    + 4

17. 12
    + 6

18. 13
    + 4

19. 14
    + 4

20. 15
    + 3

ADDITION MATH FACTS FROM 0 TO 20

1. 17
   + 1
   ___

2.   4
   +11
   ___

3.   5
   +12
   ___

4.   3
   +14
   ___

5.   2
   +15
   ___

6. 10
   + 9
   ___

7.   8
   +11
   ___

8. 11
   + 7
   ___

9.   7
   +12
   ___

10. 11
   + 9
   ___

11.   8
   +12
   ___

12. 10
   + 8
   ___

13.   5
   +13
   ___

14. 12
   + 6
   ___

15.   7
   +13
   ___

16.   5
   +14
   ___

17. 15
   + 3
   ___

18. 16
   + 4
   ___

19. 17
   + 2
   ___

20. 19
   + 1
   ___

ADDITION MATH FACTS FROM 0 TO 20

1. 14
   + 2

2. 4
   + 15

3. 3
   + 12

4. 4
   + 14

5. 3
   + 15

6. 11
   + 9

7. 7
   + 11

8. 13
   + 7

9. 6
   + 12

10. 8
    + 9

11. 5
    + 12

12. 14
    + 3

13. 5
    + 14

14. 12
    + 7

15. 3
    + 13

16. 2
    + 16

17. 15
    + 5

18. 16
    + 4

19. 17
    + 2

20. 12
    + 5

ADDITION MATH FACTS FROM 0 TO 20

1. 13
   + 4
   ____

2.   4
   +15
   ____

3.   3
   +12
   ____

4.   6
   +14
   ____

5.   3
   +15
   ____

6.   7
   + 9
   ____

7.   7
   +11
   ____

8. 13
   + 6
   ____

9.   6
   + 12
   ____

10.   8
   + 9
   ____

11.   4
   +12
   ____

12. 14
   + 5
   ____

13.   3
   +14
   ____

14. 12
   + 7
   ____

15.   3
   +13
   ____

16.   4
   + 9
   ____

17. 15
   + 5
   ____

18. 16
   + 3
   ____

19. 13
   + 2
   ____

20. 13
   + 5
   ____

SUBTRACTION MATH FACTS FROM 0 TO 20

1. 13
   − 6

2. 12
   − 8

3. 11
   − 7

4. 14
   − 7

5. 15
   − 7

6. 12
   − 6

7. 16
   − 8

8. 15
   − 9

9. 17
   − 5

10. 16
    − 5

11. 14
    − 6

12. 15
    − 5

13. 17
    − 8

14. 12
    − 5

15. 12
    − 4

16. 13
    − 7

17. 12
    − 7

18. 11
    − 4

19. 11
    − 6

20. 12
    − 3

SUBTRACTION MATH FACTS FROM 0 TO 20

1. 15
    − 6

2. 14
    − 8

3. 12
    − 7

4. 11
    − 7

5. 14
    − 7

6. 13
    − 5

7. 16
    − 9

8. 15
    − 8

9. 17
    − 6

10. 16
    − 8

11. 16
    − 6

12. 14
    − 5

13. 17
    − 9

14. 12
    − 5

15. 12
    − 3

16. 13
    − 2

17. 12
    − 8

18. 11
    − 5

19. 11
    − 2

20. 12
    − 6

SUBTRACTION MATH FACTS FROM 0 TO 20

1. 14
  − 6

2. 14
  − 5

3. 17
  − 9

4. 12
  − 5

5. 12
  − 3

6. 13
  − 7

7. 12
  − 8

8. 11
  − 7

9. 11
  − 5

10. 17
  −10

11. 15
  − 6

12. 15
  − 8

13. 12
  − 7

14. 11
  − 2

15. 14
  − 7

16. 13
  − 6

17. 16
  − 9

18. 15
  − 7

19. 17
  − 6

20. 16
  − 5

SUBTRACTION MATH FACTS FROM 0 TO 20

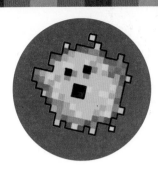

1. 16
  − 3

2. 13
  − 3

3. 14
  − 2

4. 15
  − 2

5. 17
  − 6

6. 12
  − 5

7. 14
  − 7

8. 18
  − 9

9. 16
  − 9

10. 11
  − 6

11. 15
  − 7

12. 15
  − 9

13. 13
  − 6

14. 14
  − 6

15. 17
  − 9

16. 14
  − 8

17. 16
  − 8

18. 12
  − 4

19. 12
  − 7

20. 11
  − 8

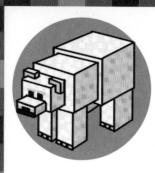

SUBTRACTION MATH FACTS FROM 0 TO 20

1. 11
   − 3

2. 13
   − 3

3. 14
   − 6

4. 15
   − 8

5. 17
   − 6

6. 12
   − 3

7. 12
   − 4

8. 16
   − 9

9. 17
   − 9

10. 11
   − 6

11. 15
   − 9

12. 14
   − 7

13. 13
   − 6

14. 12
   − 6

15. 17
   − 8

16. 14
   − 8

17. 16
   − 8

18. 12
   − 8

19. 12
   − 5

20. 11
   − 10

SUBTRACTION MATH FACTS FROM 0 TO 20

1. 20
   − 3

2. 18
   − 6

3. 17
   − 4

4. 15
   − 10

5. 20
   − 4

6. 17
   − 5

7. 16
   − 3

8. 19
   − 4

9. 20
   − 7

10. 19
    − 5

11. 16
    − 7

12. 20
    − 6

13. 20
    − 2

14. 15
    − 3

15. 17
    − 3

16. 14
    − 4

17. 19
    − 3

18. 20
    − 8

19. 15
    − 4

20. 20
    − 11

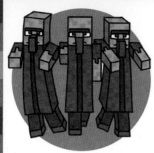

SUBTRACTION MATH FACTS FROM 0 TO 20

1. 20
   − 4

2. 19
   − 6

3. 16
   − 5

4. 18
   −10

5. 20
   − 5

6. 17
   − 3

7. 16
   − 4

8. 19
   − 2

9. 20
   − 3

10. 19
    − 4

11. 16
    − 3

12. 20
    − 7

13. 20
    − 1

14. 15
    − 2

15. 17
    − 7

16. 15
    − 4

17. 19
    − 3

18. 18
    − 5

19. 15
    − 3

20. 20
    − 9

SUBTRACTION MATH FACTS FROM 0 TO 20

1. 16
   − 4

2. 13
   − 6

3. 20
   −10

4. 18
   − 9

5. 20
   − 3

6. 17
   − 5

7. 16
   − 8

8. 19
   − 8

9. 14
   − 3

10. 18
    − 4

11. 16
    − 1

12. 20
    − 4

13. 15
    − 4

14. 15
    − 8

15. 17
    − 8

16. 15
    − 5

17. 19
    − 5

18. 18
    − 8

19. 12
    − 4

20. 20
    − 7

SUBTRACTION MATH FACTS FROM 0 TO 20

1. 16
   − 7

2. 14
   − 6

3. 13
   − 5

4. 18
   − 5

5. 20
   − 5

6. 17
   − 6

7. 16
   − 4

8. 17
   − 8

9. 19
   − 3

10. 18
    − 15

11. 16
    −10

12. 20
    − 7

13. 15
    −11

14. 14
    − 8

15. 17
    − 7

16. 15
    − 8

17. 19
    − 2

18. 18
    − 6

19. 12
    − 9

20. 20
    − 3

SUBTRACTION MATH FACTS FROM 0 TO 20

1. 16
    − 8

2. 14
    − 9

3. 13
    − 3

4. 12
    − 5

5. 11
    − 5

6. 11
    − 4

7. 16
    − 7

8. 17
    − 8

9. 15
    − 9

10. 18
    −10

11. 16
    − 5

12. 20
    −10

13. 15
    − 5

14. 14
    − 6

15. 17
    − 9

16. 15
    − 7

17. 13
    − 6

18. 14
    − 8

19. 12
    − 4

20. 13
    − 7

MIXED ADDITION & SUBTRACTION FROM 0 TO 20

1. 3
    + 8

2. 16
    − 5

3. 4
    + 7

4. 18
    − 9

5. 6
    + 6

6. 8
    − 6

7. 8
    + 5

8. 7
    − 7

9. 9
    + 9

10. 12
     − 8

11. 5
     + 9

12. 15
     − 7

13. 7
     + 9

14. 8
     − 4

15. 9
     + 3

16. 8
     − 7

17. 8
     + 8

18. 12
     − 9

19. 8
     + 3

20. 11
     − 6

MIXED ADDITION & SUBTRACTION FROM 0 TO 20

1. 8
    + 5

2. 11
    - 3

3. 8
    + 7

4. 17
    - 8

5. 7
    + 6

6. 13
    - 6

7. 6
    + 6

8. 12
    - 5

9. 7
    + 5

10. 14
    - 8

11. 5
    + 6

12. 14
    - 7

13. 3
    + 8

14. 17
    - 9

15. 9
    + 3

16. 9
    + 9

17. 12
    + 8

18. 7
    + 9

19. 12
    - 3

20. 5
    + 8

MIXED ADDITION & SUBTRACTION FROM 0 TO 20

1. $9 + 7$

2. $18 - 8$

3. $20 - 5$

4. $12 + 8$

5. $9 + 6$

6. $8 + 7$

7. $16 - 7$

8. $20 - 9$

9. $4 + 7$

10. $9 + 5$

11. $15 - 9$

12. $6 + 8$

13. $7 + 6$

14. $13 - 6$

15. $6 + 6$

16. $14 - 6$

17. $18 - 9$

18. $7 + 5$

19. $5 + 6$

20. $7 + 7$

MIXED ADDITION & SUBTRACTION FROM 0 TO 20

1. $\begin{array}{r} 9 \\ + 2 \\ \hline \end{array}$

2. $\begin{array}{r} 8 \\ + 3 \\ \hline \end{array}$

3. $\begin{array}{r} 17 \\ - 9 \\ \hline \end{array}$

4. $\begin{array}{r} 16 \\ - 5 \\ \hline \end{array}$

5. $\begin{array}{r} 9 \\ + 7 \\ \hline \end{array}$

6. $\begin{array}{r} 12 \\ - 5 \\ \hline \end{array}$

7. $\begin{array}{r} 5 \\ + 7 \\ \hline \end{array}$

8. $\begin{array}{r} 9 \\ + 9 \\ \hline \end{array}$

9. $\begin{array}{r} 12 \\ - 4 \\ \hline \end{array}$

10. $\begin{array}{r} 7 \\ + 7 \\ \hline \end{array}$

11. $\begin{array}{r} 5 \\ + 9 \\ \hline \end{array}$

12. $\begin{array}{r} 16 \\ - 8 \\ \hline \end{array}$

13. $\begin{array}{r} 7 \\ + 6 \\ \hline \end{array}$

14. $\begin{array}{r} 8 \\ + 4 \\ \hline \end{array}$

15. $\begin{array}{r} 14 \\ - 8 \\ \hline \end{array}$

16. $\begin{array}{r} 4 \\ + 7 \\ \hline \end{array}$

17. $\begin{array}{r} 12 \\ - 9 \\ \hline \end{array}$

18. $\begin{array}{r} 4 \\ + 9 \\ \hline \end{array}$

19. $\begin{array}{r} 15 \\ - 7 \\ \hline \end{array}$

20. $\begin{array}{r} 7 \\ + 8 \\ \hline \end{array}$

MYSTERY NUMBER ADDITION

Fill in the missing number to complete the equation.

Examples:

1.
$$3 + \boxed{4} = 7$$

2.
$$\boxed{6} + 4 = 10$$

3.
$$6 + \boxed{} = 8$$

4.
$$5 + \boxed{} = 8$$

5.
$$4 + \boxed{} = 8$$

6.
$$\boxed{} + 5 = 9$$

7.
$$5 + \boxed{} = 10$$

8.
$$2 + 7 = \boxed{}$$

9.
$$\boxed{} + 6 = 9$$

10.
$$2 + \boxed{} = 5$$

11.
$$\boxed{} + 3 = 6$$

12.
$$7 + \boxed{} = 10$$

13.
$$4 + 4 = \boxed{}$$

14.
$$9 + \boxed{} = 10$$

15.
$$\boxed{} + 1 = 8$$

16.
$$\boxed{} + 2 = 6$$

17.
$$2 + \boxed{} = 7$$

18.
$$2 + 4 = \boxed{}$$

19.
$$\boxed{} + 3 = 9$$

20.
$$8 + \boxed{} = 10$$

MYSTERY NUMBER ADDITION

Fill in the missing number to complete the equation.

1. 13
    + ☐
    ———
    20

2. ☐
    + 4
    ———
    16

3. 6
    + ☐
    ———
    14

4. 5
    + ☐
    ———
    13

5. 4
    + ☐
    ———
    12

6. ☐
    + 5
    ———
    12

7. 5
    + ☐
    ———
    11

8. 2
    + 7
    ———
    ☐

9. ☐
    + 3
    ———
    12

10. 2
    + ☐
    ———
    10

11. ☐
    + 3
    ———
    12

12. 7
    + 7
    ———
    ☐

13. 4
    +16
    ———
    ☐

14. 9
    + ☐
    ———
    14

15. ☐
    + 7
    ———
    12

16. ☐
    + 7
    ———
    13

17. 6
    + ☐
    ———
    12

18. 8
    + 6
    ———
    ☐

19. ☐
    + 6
    ———
    15

20. 8
    + ☐
    ———
    18

MYSTERY NUMBER SUBTRACTION

Fill in the missing number to complete the equation.

1. 10
    − ☐
    ───
    7

2. ☐
    − 4
    ───
    4

3. 6
    − ☐
    ───
    3

4. 8
    − ☐
    ───
    5

5. 4
    − ☐
    ───
    4

6. ☐
    − 5
    ───
    4

7. 5
    − ☐
    ───
    3

8. 2
    − 1
    ───
    ☐

9. ☐
    − 6
    ───
    4

10. 5
    − ☐
    ───
    1

11. ☐
    − 2
    ───
    8

12. 7
    − ☐
    ───
    2

13. 7
    − 4
    ───
    ☐

14. 9
    − ☐
    ───
    5

15. ☐
    − 1
    ───
    8

16. ☐
    − 2
    ───
    6

17. 9
    − ☐
    ───
    7

18. 4
    − 2
    ───
    ☐

19. ☐
    − 2
    ───
    8

20. 8
    − ☐
    ───
    2

MYSTERY NUMBER SUBTRACTION

Fill in the missing number to complete the equation.

1. 13
    - ▢
    ――
    10

2. ▢
    - 4
    ――
    16

3. 16
    - ▢
    ――
    8

4. 15
    - ▢
    ――
    10

5. 14
    - ▢
    ――
    12

6. ▢
    - 5
    ――
    6

7. 12
    - ▢
    ――
    7

8. 12
    - 9
    ――
    ▢

9. ▢
    - 6
    ――
    11

10. 13
    - ▢
    ――
    8

11. ▢
    - 3
    ――
    12

12. 17
    - 7
    ――
    ▢

13. 16
    - 4
    ――
    ▢

14. 19
    - ▢
    ――
    15

15. ▢
    - 3
    ――
    11

16. ▢
    - 6
    ――
    7

17. 18
    - ▢
    ――
    13

18. 18
    - 6
    ――
    ▢

19. ▢
    - 6
    ――
    14

20. 18
    - ▢
    ――
    9

ANSWER KEY

PAGE 111

1. 7
2. 6
3. 9
4. 8
5. 10
6. 10
7. 10
8. 6
9. 8
10. 5
11. 8
12. 9
13. 6
14. 9
15. 9
16. 7
17. 10
18. 8
19. 5
20. 7

PAGE 112

1. 10
2. 7
3. 8
4. 8
5. 10
6. 9
7. 10
8. 5
9. 6
10. 7
11. 8
12. 9
13. 9
14. 8
15. 9
16. 7
17. 9
18. 8
19. 7
20. 4

PAGE 113

1. 2
2. 2
3. 3
4. 4
5. 3
6. 6
7. 4
8. 7
9. 3
10. 5
11. 7
12. 5
13. 2
14. 5
15. 4
16. 2
17. 6
18. 3
19. 5
20. 2

PAGE 114

1. 8
2. 4
3. 4
4. 3
5. 0
6. 6
7. 4
8. 7
9. 3
10. 1
11. 5
12. 5
13. 2
14. 5
15. 4
16. 2
17. 7
18. 3
19. 5
20. 2

PAGE 115

1. 6
2. 3
3. 5
4. 3
5. 1
6. 8
7. 4
8. 2
9. 7
10. 3
11. 3
12. 8
13. 4
14. 2
15. 4
16. 4
17. 6
18. 8
19. 4
20. 5

PAGE 116

1. 2
2. 2
3. 3
4. 3
5. 1
6. 4
7. 2
8. 5
9. 5
10. 3
11. 3
12. 4
13. 8
14. 5
15. 4
16. 3
17. 6
18. 6
19. 8
20. 2

PAGE 117

1. 1
2. 2
3. 2
4. 5
5. 0
6. 2
7. 4
8. 4
9. 0
10. 1
11. 0
12. 1
13. 0
14. 2
15. 3
16. 3
17. 0
18. 5
19. 3
20. 2

PAGE 118

1. 16
2. 16
3. 19
4. 12
5. 15
6. 13
7. 15
8. 18
9. 13
10. 14
11. 14
12. 14
13. 12
14. 11
15. 12
16. 11
17. 13
18. 15
19. 11
20. 13

PAGE 119

1. 11
2. 11
3. 11
4. 11
5. 12
6. 13
7. 15
8. 18
9. 13
10. 14
11. 14
12. 14
13. 12
14. 12
15. 12
16. 11
17. 13
18. 12
19. 11
20. 13

PAGE 120

1. 15
2. 11
3. 11
4. 11
5. 14
6. 13
7. 15
8. 18
9. 13
10. 12
11. 14
12. 14
13. 12
14. 12
15. 12
16. 11
17. 13
18. 12
19. 14
20. 12

PAGE 121

1. 11
2. 11
3. 11
4. 12
5. 12
6. 14
7. 13
8. 15
9. 18
10. 12
11. 14
12. 14
13. 16
14. 12
15. 12
16. 15
17. 16
18. 13
19. 11
20. 11

PAGE 122

1. 12
2. 16
3. 15
4. 16
5. 18
6. 12
7. 14
8. 11
9. 12
10. 12
11. 11
12. 13
13. 16
14. 12
15. 11
16. 13
17. 15
18. 12
19. 11
20. 13

PAGE 123

1. 13
2. 12
3. 16
4. 17
5. 13
6. 14
7. 12
8. 15
9. 12
10. 12
11. 11
12. 11
13. 11
14. 11
15. 12
16. 18
17. 16
18. 16
19. 20
20. 13

PAGE 124

1. 14
2. 16
3. 18
4. 18
5. 15
6. 18
7. 16
8. 18
9. 12
10. 18
11. 17
12. 18
13. 18
14. 15
15. 13
16. 15
17. 18
18. 17
19. 18
20. 18

PAGE 125

1. 18
2. 15
3. 17
4. 17
5. 17
6. 19
7. 19
8. 18
9. 19
10. 20
11. 20
12. 18
13. 18
14. 18
15. 20
16. 19
17. 18
18. 20
19. 19
20. 20

PAGE 126

1. 16
2. 19
3. 15
4. 18
5. 18
6. 20
7. 18
8. 20
9. 18
10. 17
11. 17
12. 17
13. 19
14. 19
15. 16
16. 18
17. 20
18. 20
19. 19
20. 17

PAGE 127

1. 17
2. 19
3. 15
4. 20
5. 18
6. 16
7. 18
8. 19
9. 18
10. 17
11. 16
12. 19
13. 17
14. 19
15. 16
16. 13
17. 20
18. 19
19. 15
20. 18

PAGE 128

1. 7
2. 4
3. 4
4. 7
5. 8
6. 6
7. 8
8. 6
9. 12
10. 11
11. 8
12. 10
13. 9
14. 7
15. 8
16. 6
17. 5
18. 7
19. 5
20. 9

PAGE 129

1. 9
2. 6
3. 5
4. 4
5. 7
6. 8
7. 7
8. 7
9. 11
10. 8
11. 10
12. 9
13. 8
14. 7
15. 9
16. 11
17. 4
18. 6
19. 9
20. 6

PAGE 130

1. 8
2. 9
3. 8
4. 7
5. 9
6. 6
7. 4
8. 4
9. 6
10. 7
11. 9
12. 7
13. 5
14. 9
15. 7
16. 7
17. 7
18. 8
19. 11
20. 11

PAGE 131

1. 13
2. 10
3. 12
4. 13
5. 11
6. 7
7. 7
8. 9
9. 7
10. 5
11. 8
12. 6
13. 7
14. 8
15. 8
16. 6
17. 8
18. 8
19. 5
20. 3

PAGE 132

1. 8
2. 10
3. 8
4. 7
5. 11
6. 9
7. 8
8. 7
9. 8
10. 5
11. 6
12. 7
13. 7
14. 6
15. 9
16. 6
17. 8
18. 4
19. 7
20. 1

PAGE 133

1. 17
2. 12
3. 13
4. 5
5. 16
6. 12
7. 13
8. 15
9. 13
10. 14
11. 9
12. 14
13. 18
14. 12
15. 14
16. 10
17. 16
18. 12
19. 11
20. 9

PAGE 134

1. 16
2. 13
3. 11
4. 8
5. 15
6. 14
7. 12
8. 17
9. 17
10. 15
11. 13
12. 13
13. 19
14. 13
15. 10
16. 11
17. 16
18. 13
19. 12
20. 11

PAGE 135

1. 12
2. 7
3. 10
4. 9
5. 17
6. 12
7. 8
8. 11
9. 11
10. 14
11. 15
12. 16
13. 11
14. 7
15. 9
16. 10
17. 14
18. 10
19. 8
20. 13

PAGE 136

1. 9
2. 8
3. 8
4. 13
5. 15
6. 11
7. 12
8. 9
9. 16
10. 3
11. 6
12. 13
13. 4
14. 6
15. 10
16. 7
17. 17
18. 12
19. 3
20. 17

PAGE 137

1. 8
2. 5
3. 10
4. 7
5. 6
6. 7
7. 9
8. 9
9. 6
10. 8
11. 11
12. 10
13. 10
14. 8
15. 8
16. 8
17. 7
18. 6
19. 8
20. 6

PAGE 138

1. 11
2. 11
3. 11
4. 9
5. 12
6. 2
7. 13
8. 0
9. 18
10. 4
11. 14
12. 8
13. 16
14. 4
15. 12
16. 1
17. 16
18. 3
19. 11
20. 5

PAGE 139

1. 13
2. 8
3. 15
4. 9
5. 13
6. 7
7. 12
8. 7
9. 12
10. 6
11. 11
12. 7
13. 11
14. 8
15. 12
16. 18
17. 20
18. 16
19. 9
20. 13

PAGE 140

1. 16
2. 10
3. 15
4. 20
5. 15
6. 15
7. 9
8. 11
9. 11
10. 14
11. 6
12. 14
13. 13
14. 7
15. 12
16. 8
17. 9
18. 12
19. 11
20. 14

PAGE 141

1. 11
2. 11
3. 8
4. 11
5. 16
6. 7
7. 12
8. 18
9. 8
10. 14
11. 14
12. 8
13. 13
14. 12
15. 6
16. 11
17. 3
18. 13
19. 8
20. 15

PAGE 142

1. 4
2. 6
3. 2
4. 3
5. 4
6. 4
7. 5
8. 9
9. 3
10. 3
11. 3
12. 3
13. 8
14. 1
15. 7
16. 4
17. 5
18. 6
19. 6
20. 2

PAGE 143

1. 7
2. 12
3. 8
4. 8
5. 8
6. 7
7. 6
8. 9
9. 9
10. 8
11. 9
12. 14
13. 20
14. 5
15. 5
16. 6
17. 6
18. 14
19. 9
20. 10

PAGE 144

1. 3
2. 8
3. 3
4. 3
5. 0
6. 9
7. 2
8. 1
9. 10
10. 4
11. 10
12. 5
13. 3
14. 4
15. 9
16. 8
17. 2
18. 2
19. 10
20. 6

PAGE 145

1. 3
2. 20
3. 8
4. 5
5. 2
6. 11
7. 5
8. 3
9. 17
10. 5
11. 15
12. 10
13. 12
14. 4
15. 14
16. 13
17. 5
18. 12
19. 20
20. 9

GAMES AND PUZZLES FOR
MINECRAFTERS

AMAZING ACTIVITIES

STEVE SAYS...

If you have ever played the game Simon Says, then you know how this game works: **follow only the directions that begin with "Steve says"** *to reveal a fun fact for Minecrafters.*

	1	2	3	4	5
A	SPIDERS	ONE	CREEPERS	CREATE	MAGENTA
B	WERE	SILVERFISH	MAKE	VILLAGERS	THE
C	OCELOT	RESULT	CONSTRUCT	GREEN	OF
D	PINK	IS	A	FOREST	SAVANNA
E	CODING	PURPLE	THE	MISTAKE	BE

1. **Steve says**, "Cross off all the Mobs in Row B and in Column 1."

2. **Steve says**, "Cross off all colors."

3. **Steve says**, "Cross off all biomes."

4. Cross off nouns (people, places, things) in Column 4.

5. **Steve says**, "Cross off synonyms of 'build' in Columns 3 and 4."

6. **Steve says**, "Cross off words with four or fewer letters in Column 2 and in Row E."

7. **Steve says**, "Read the remaining words to reveal a fact about the game."

THE MIRROR'S IMAGE

Circle letters on the top half of the grid that have correct mirror images on the bottom half. Write the circled letters in order on the spaces provided to reveal a cool fact about Endermen.

```
E I M N D N E O R T M E K N W I E R E D
C A L D L I E D F N A G R Y L A N O D E
U R P S B E U Z F O R Z L E T E H E P E
N E D W R A S S C R O E A T N E Y D O U
———————————————————————————————————————
N U D M S A P S C R E A T O E P D T E
R R E S B E T A T O R B U T H E O E
C A T T T A E D E A R R T A N A D E
E P U N D S E S R T W E E N M S E R E O
```

_ _ _ _ _ _ _ _ _   _ _ _ _   _ _ _ _ _ _

" _ _ _ _ _ _ _ _ _ _ _ "   _ _ _ _   _ _

_ _ _   _ _ _   _ _ _ _ _

155

CITY SLICKER

A highly skilled Minecrafter built the first city below. She logged back in later and made ten changes to her city. Look at the second city on the opposite page. Can you identify all ten changes?

TAKE A GUESS

Write the answers to the clues on the numbered spaces, one letter on each blank. Then transfer the letters to the boxes with the same numbers. A few have already been done for you! If you fill in the boxes correctly, you'll reveal something very useful for Minecrafters.

The way out

$$\frac{}{10} \quad \frac{x}{2} \quad \frac{}{6} \quad \frac{}{15}$$

This grows on ears and is sometimes popped

$$\frac{}{9} \quad \frac{}{12} \quad \frac{r}{5} \quad \frac{}{8}$$

A kind of tree

$$\frac{p}{11} \quad \frac{}{13} \quad \frac{}{14} \quad \frac{}{1}$$

To leak through

$$\frac{s}{16} \quad \frac{}{4} \quad \frac{}{7} \quad \frac{}{3}$$

1	2 x	3	4	5 r	6	7	8	9	10

11 p	12	13	14	15	16 s

ENCHANTED CHEST

This End City chest is enchanted. To open it, you must press all nine buttons just once, in the correct order.

Follow the directions on the buttons. For instance, 2D means you must move your finger two buttons down. R=right. L=left. U=up. To open the chest, you must land on the F button last.

Which button do you have to press first to land on the F button last?

SEE AND SOLVE

In this crossword puzzle, you get to figure out where each word fits! Use the picture clues to guess the word answers, then see where each word fits best. If you fill in the puzzle correctly, you'll get a funny answer to the question below!

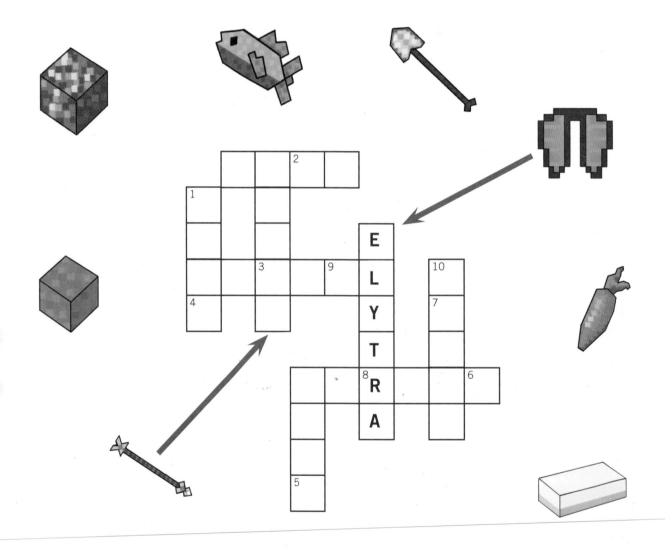

What happens when blazes are promoted to managers?

$\overline{6}$ $\overline{4}$ $\overline{9}$ $\overline{5}$ $\overline{1}$ $\overline{10}$ $\overline{8}$ $\overline{9}$ $\overline{9}$ $\overline{2}$ $\overline{9}$ $\overline{8}$ $\overline{5}$ $\overline{3}$ $\overline{7}$ $\overline{9}$

HOME SWEET BIOME

Find and circle the names of fourteen Minecraft biomes in the wordfind below. They might be forward, backward, up, down, or diagonal.

DEEP OCEAN

DESERT

EXTREME HILLS

FROZEN RIVER

JUNGLE

MUSHROOM ISLAND

NETHER

PLAINS

ROOFED FOREST

SAVANNA

STONE BEACH

SWAMPLAND

TAIGA

THE END

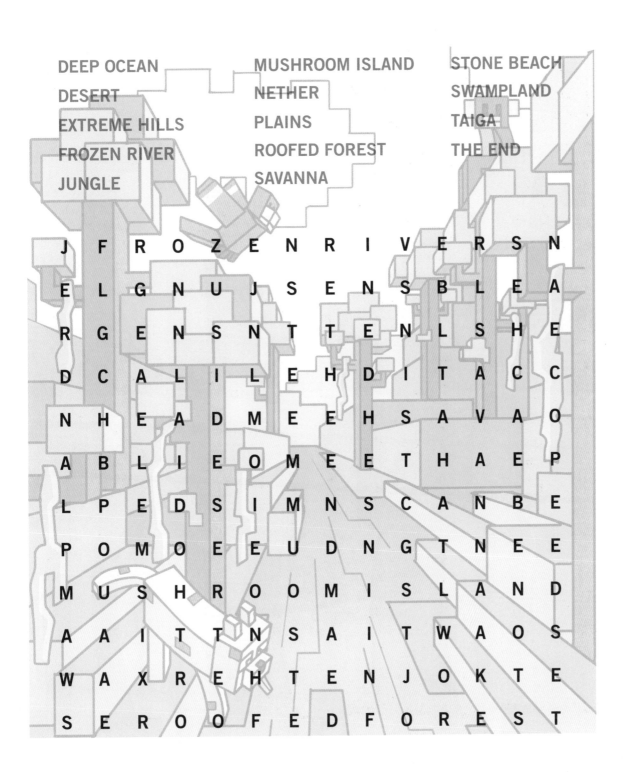

```
J F R O Z E N R I V E R S N
E L G N U J S E N S B L E A
R G E N S N T T E N L S H E
D C A L I L E H D I T A C C
N H E A D M E E H S A V A O
A B L I E O M E E T H A E P
L P E D S I M N S C A N B E
P O M O E E U D N G T N E E
M U S H R O O M I S L A N D
A A I T T N S A I T W A O S
W A X R E H T E N J O K T E
S E R O O F E D F O R E S T
```

CREEPER TWINS

Only two of these creepers are exactly the same. Which two are identical?

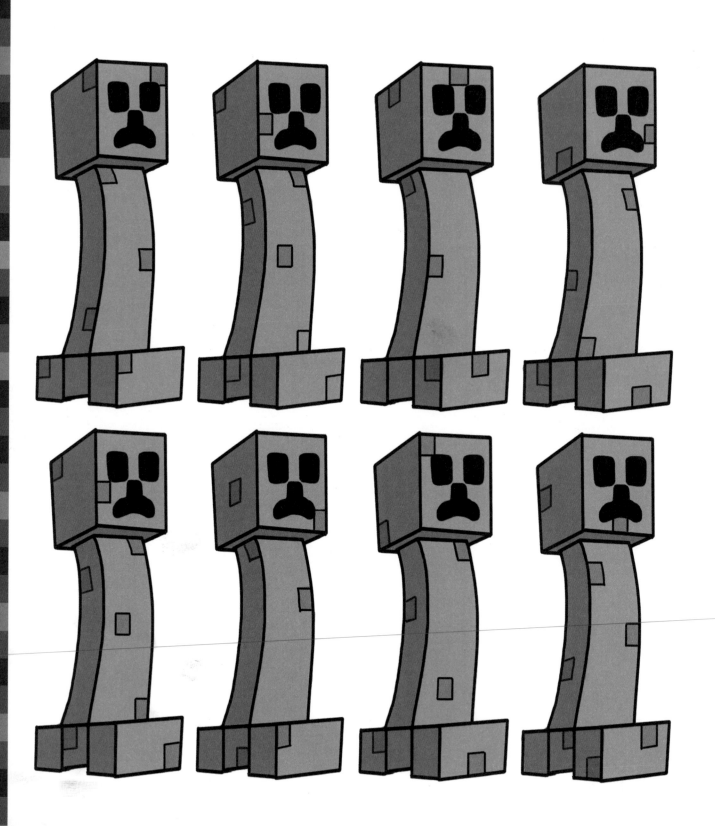

CIRCLE OF TRUTH: CRAFTING CLUE

Start at the ▼. Write every third letter on the spaces below to reveal a truth that all Minecrafters should know.

N D E G I S E A T S M H T O E T N S O D T O M R L A O S K

D _ _ _ _ _ _ _   _ _ _ _ _   _ _ _

_ _ _ _ _ _ _ _ _   _ _ _ _

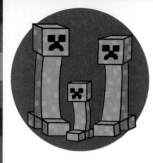

MOB SCENE

Write answers to the clues in the boxes. Read the highlighted boxes downward to reveal a phrase that describes a common Mob scene. Need a hint? The answers are scrambled around the border.

SONIE   RACESH

1. To look for something
2. Someone with mad skills
3. Horses and pigs eat these
4. Another word for a Minecrafter
5. The opposite of *input*
6. Use this to ride a pig
7. The eye of this is poisonous and used in brewing
8. Another word for *sound*
9. Use this to spawn a chicken

PALSEP

TOPUTU

DASLED

REVPAL

1.
2.
3.
4.
5.
6.
7.
8.
9.

GEG   REPEXT   DRISPE

SQUARED UP: MOBS IN EVERY QUARTER

Each of the four mobs in this puzzle can appear only once in each row, each column, and the four inside boxes.

B = BABY ZOMBIE VILLAGERS

C = CREEPER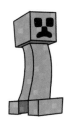

G = GHAST

S = SKELETON

G			B
B	S		
		B	S
	B		G

WATCHTOWER QUEST

Can you find your way back home to where you built the watchtower?

START

A CURE FOR WHAT AILS YOU

Boxes connected by lines contain the same letter. Some letters are given; others have to be guessed. Fill in all the boxes to reveal a piece of gaming advice.

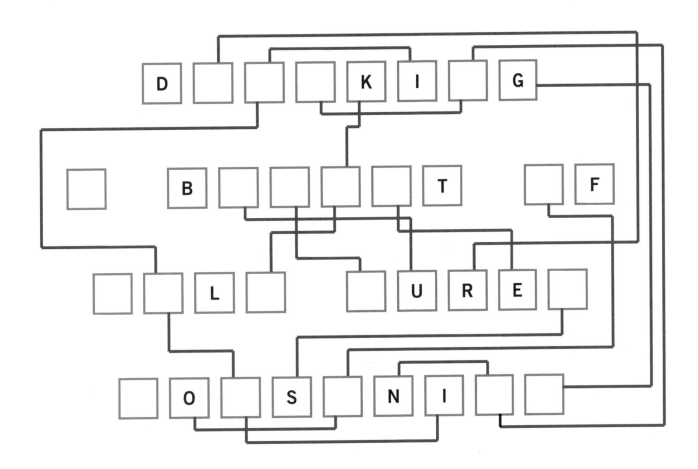

YOU CAN DRAW IT: WOLF

Use the grid to copy the picture one square at a time. Examine the lines in each small square in the top grid then transfer those lines to the corresponding square in the bottom grid. When you finish, you'll have drawn a wolf all your own!

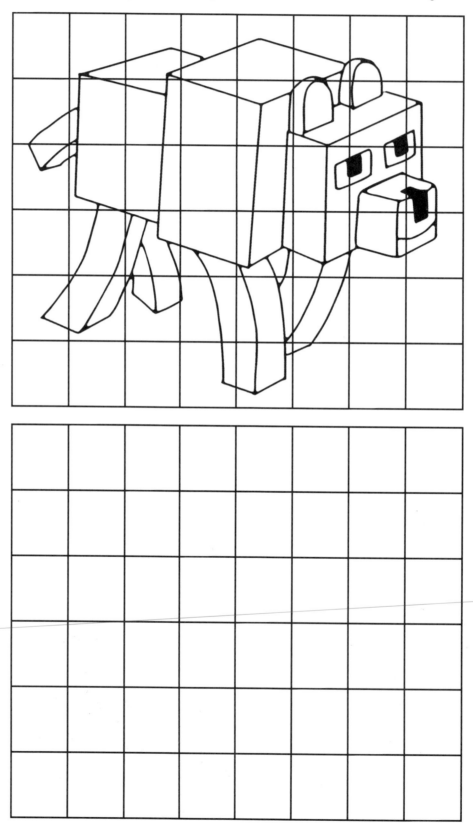

PIECE IT TOGETHER

Identify the seven green puzzle pieces that fit the shapes in the rectangle. Watch out! Pieces might be rotated or flipped. Write the letters of the correct pieces on each space. Not all the pieces will be used.

Read the letters you wrote to reveal the answer to the following question: **What mobs make Steve and Alex tremble in fear?**

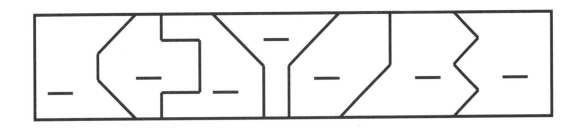

PICK, THE RIGHT TOOL!

There are thirteen pickaxes hidden in this toolshed. Can you pick them all out?

TOOL CHEST

Find and circle the names of nine Minecrafting tools in the letters. They might be forward, backward, up, down, or diagonal. Watch out! Every T, O, and L has been chipped away and replaced by a pickaxe. Can you find all nine tools?

CLOCK

COMPASS

FISHING ROD

FLINT AND STEEL

IRON AXE

LEAD

PICKAXE

SHEARS

SHOVEL

```
G  K  C  ⛏  ⛏  C  W  E  D  ⛏  I  S  U
I  M  P  E  D  ⛏  I  R  ⛏  N  A  X  E
⛏  J  B  ⛏  S  M  S  P  A  M  ⛏  F  H
V  U  P  D  N  P  F  ⛏  X  S  G  B  ⛏
F  ⛏  I  N  ⛏  A  N  D  S  ⛏  E  E  ⛏
P  C  C  R  E  S  Y  U  B  Q  V  N  W
D  W  K  ⛏  K  S  H  A  U  ⛏  F  C  I
A  ⛏  A  U  H  V  C  E  H  K  Y  J  R
E  K  X  I  ⛏  A  N  S  A  R  ⛏  F  ⛏
⛏  X  E  M  U  H  ⛏  U  C  R  M  E  I
A  ⛏  S  D  ⛏  R  G  N  I  H  S  I  F
```

FIND THE PORTAL

Four players are racing to find the End portal. Only one will make it. Follow each player's path, under and over crossing paths, to discover who gets there and who hits a dead end.

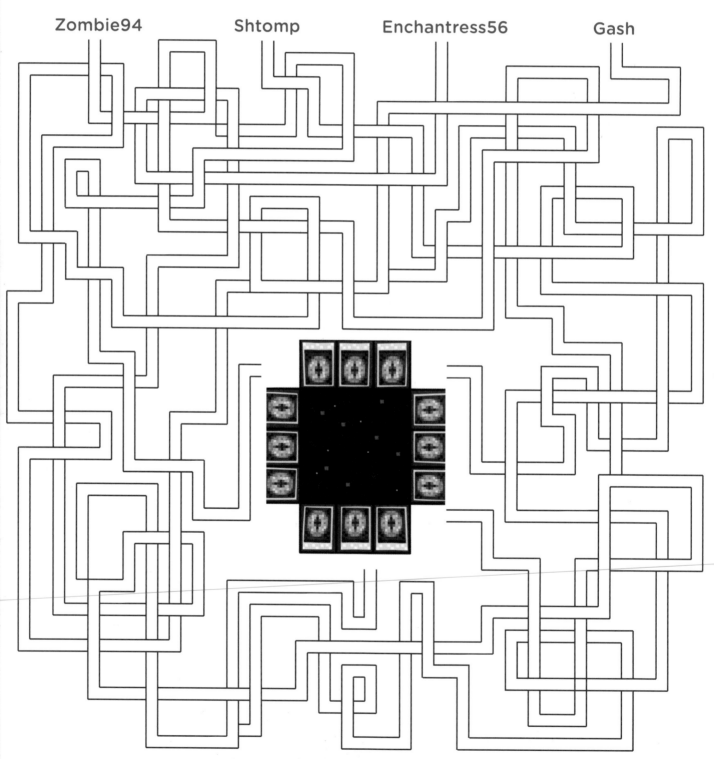

Zombie94   Shtomp   Enchantress56   Gash

CROSSWORD CLUE FINDER

Use the pictures and arrows to help you fill in this crossword picture puzzle. Some words can fit in more than one location, so choose carefully!

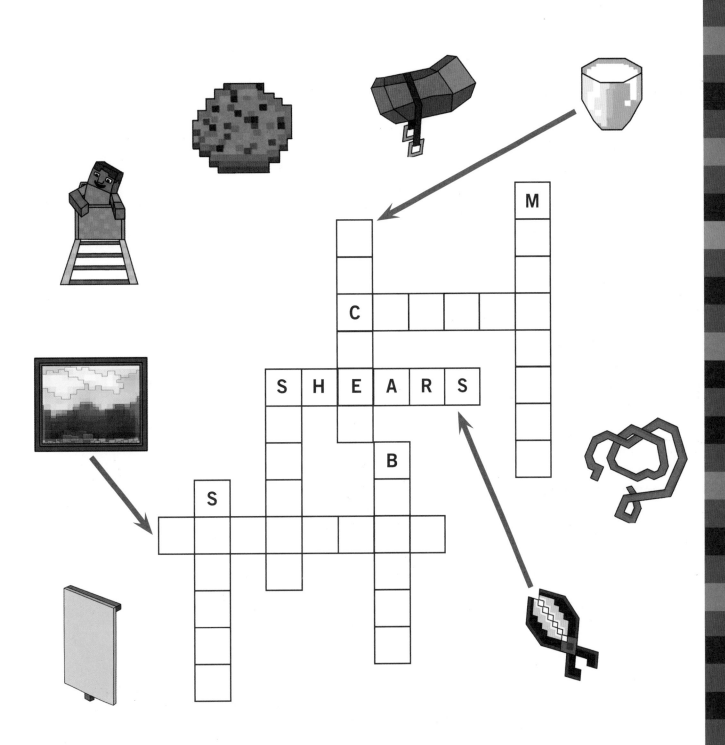

SEE THE SEA

These two pictures seem identical, but there are eleven differences between them. How many can you see?

POWER PLAY: MYSTERY WORD

Every word in Column B contains the same letters as a word in Column A, plus one letter. Draw a line between word "matches," then write the extra letter on the space provided. Unscramble the column of letters to reveal a powerful resource for Minecrafters.

COLUMN A	COLUMN B	EXTRA LETTER
Points	Steve	__
Healer	Diamond	__
Vest	Armor	__
Meander	Hardcore	__
Mentor	Potions	O
Domain	Monster	__
Roam	Enderman	__
Orchard	Leather	__

__ __ __ __ __ __ __ __ __

SURVIVAL MAZE

Find your way through this maze from Start to Finish without bumping into a ghast, creeper, zombie, or skeleton.

Start

Finish

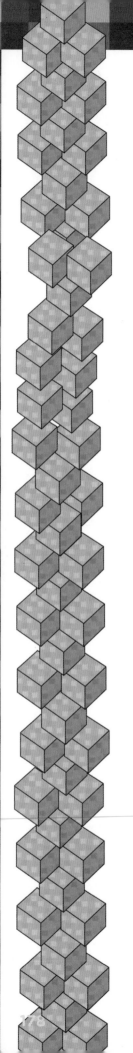

BLOCKED!

The names of fourteen Minecraft blocks are hidden below. They might be forward, backward, up, down, or diagonal. For an added challenge, some of the letters are blocked: every D, I, R, and T has been replaced by a 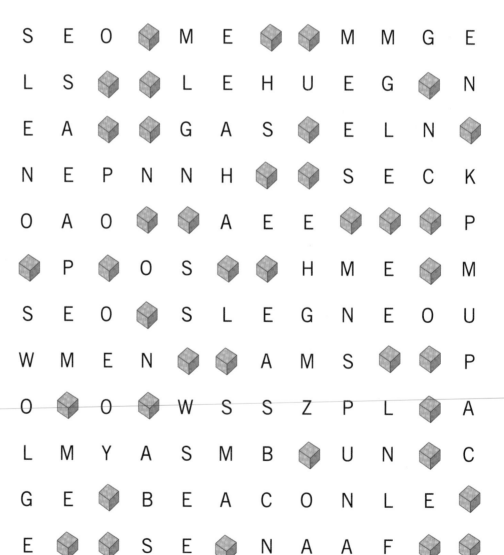. Can you find all fourteen block names?

ANDESITE   GRANITE   OBSIDIAN

BEACON   LAPIS LAZULI   PRISMARINE

DIORITE   MONSTER EGG   PUMPKIN

EMERALD   MUSHROOM   SPONGE

GLOWSTONE   NETHER WART

S	E	O	⬛	M	E	⬛	⬛	M	M	G	E
L	S	⬛	⬛	L	E	H	U	E	G	⬛	N
E	A	⬛	⬛	G	A	S	⬛	E	L	N	⬛
N	E	P	N	N	H	⬛	⬛	S	E	C	K
O	A	O	⬛	⬛	A	E	E	⬛	⬛	⬛	P
⬛	P	⬛	O	S	⬛	⬛	H	M	E	⬛	M
S	E	O	⬛	S	L	E	G	N	E	O	U
W	M	E	N	⬛	⬛	A	M	S	⬛	⬛	P
O	⬛	O	⬛	W	S	S	Z	P	L	⬛	A
L	M	Y	A	S	M	B	⬛	U	N	⬛	C
G	E	⬛	B	E	A	C	O	N	L	E	⬛
E	⬛	⬛	S	E	⬛	N	A	A	F	⬛	⬛

CONNECT THE DOTS: HOSTILE MOB

Connect the dots to discover the original boss mob!

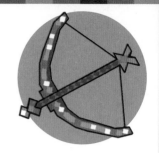

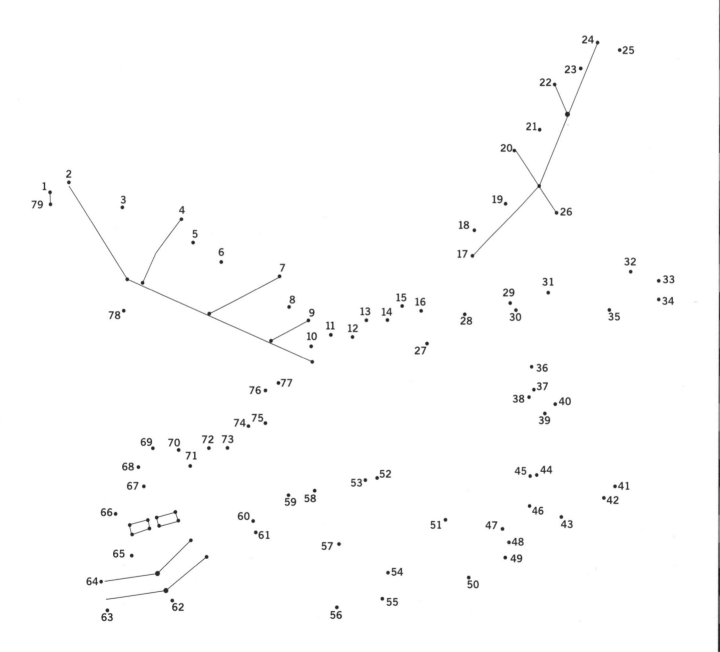

MIXED UP

Write the answers to the clues on the spaces, one letter on each blank. Then transfer the letters to the boxes below that have the same numbers. If you fill in the boxes correctly, you'll reveal something Alex loves to brew.

Big smile

___ ___ ___ ___
9 6 13 3

12 o'clock (mid-day)

___ ___ ___ ___
15 11 14 8

Pork chop source

___ ___ ___
10 2 4

Ceramic square on a bathroom floor

___ ___ ___ ___
12 7 1 5

1	2	3	4	5	6	7	8	9

10	11	12	13	14	15

A SMALL PROBLEM

Every word in Column B contains the same letters as a word in Column A, plus one extra letter. Draw a line between word "matches," then write the extra letter on the space provided.

Unscramble the column of letters to reveal a small problem for Minecrafters.

Column A	Column B	
Drips	Slime	M
Wasp	Tamed	__
Lies	Spider	__
Unreal	Hostile	__
Thaw	Neutral	__
Hotels	Pearl	__
Meat	Wheat	__
Trace	Spawn	__
Leap	Create	__

__ __ __ __ __ __ __ __ __

CRACK THE CODE

You don't need a pickaxe to crack this code, just your brain.

Use the code below to find the answer to the joke:

Why did Steve attack the cake with a stick?

W	P	O	C	A	S	T	B	K	U	D	I	N	E	R

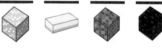

182

ALPHA CODE

The answer to the joke will be revealed as you add letters to the empty boxes that come before, between, or after the given letters in the alphabet. If you get to Z, start all over again with A. The first letter has already been written for you.

Why was the Ender Dragon book a flop?

B	E	C	A	U	S	E		I	T
C	F	D	B	V	T	F		J	U
D	G	E	C	W	U	G		K	V

R	S	Z	Q	S	D	C
S	T	A	R	T	E	D
T	U	B	S	U	F	E

Y	R		R	F	C		C	L	B
Z	S		S	G	D		D	M	C
A	T		T	H	E		E	N	D

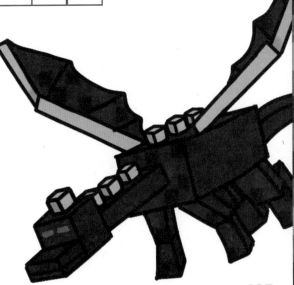

GRAB AND GO CHALLENGE

Pick up every single experience orb in this maze, but do it quickly to escape the zombie chasing you. You'll need to draw a line from Start to Stop that passes through every orb once. Your line can go up, down, left, or right, but not diagonally. On your mark, get set, go!

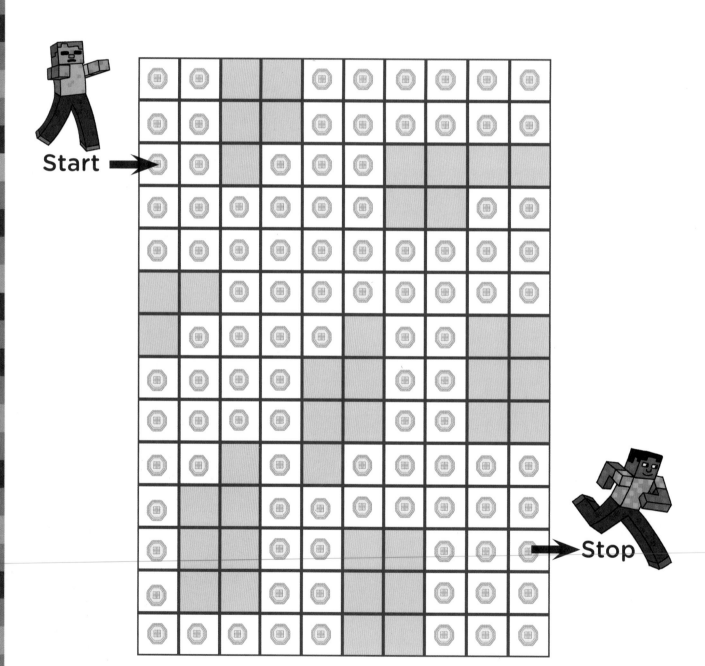

Start ➤

➤ Stop

WORD MINE

Find and circle the names of fourteen raw materials in the wordfind. They might be forward, backward, up, down, or diagonal. Watch out! Every R, A, and W has been replaced with a redstone block.

BLAZE ROD
DIAMOND
DRAGON'S BREATH
ENDER PEARL
FEATHER

FLINT
GLOWSTONE DUST
GOLD INGOT
LEATHER
MAGMA CREAM

NETHER WART
PRISMARINE SHARD
REDSTONE
STRING

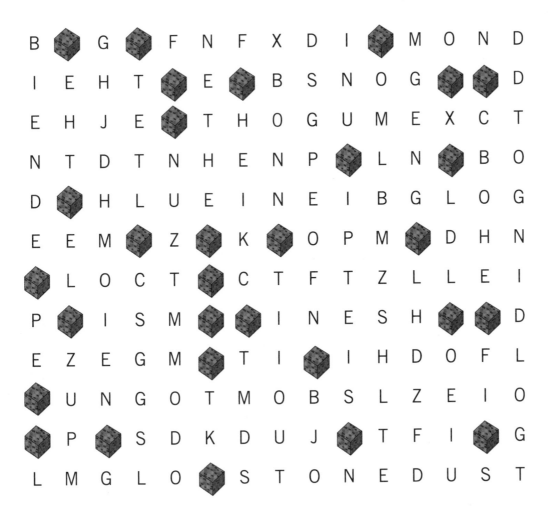

CIRCLE OF TRUTH: FUN FACT

Start at the ▼. Write every third letter on the spaces to reveal a Minecrafting secret.

↓

C N Y A A O T C U S H C I E A T S N S T I O I O N F P I A E T

Y _ _ _ , _ _ _ _ _ _ _

_ _ _ _ _ _ _ _ _ _ _

ZOMBIE TWINS

Only two of these zombies are exactly the same. Which two are identical?

CAN YOU DIG IT?

Turn MINE into ORES one letter at a time. The answer to each clue looks like the word above it, except one letter is different. If you get stuck, try working from the bottom up.

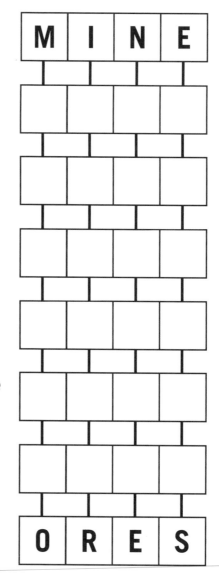

| M | I | N | E |

A silent actor

Ten-cent coin

Darkens slowly

Points at a target

Where elbows are found

Greek god of war

| O | R | E | S |

SQUARED UP: FARM MOBS

Each of the four mobs in this puzzle can appear only once in each row, each column, and the four inside boxes. Fill in the remaining empty boxes with the first letter of a mob shown below.

C = COW

P = PIG

H = HORSE

S = SHEEP

S	H		P
	C		
C		S	
H			C

GROW WITH THE FLOW

Find the flow of letters that spell out a fun fact for Minecrafters. Start with the corner letter, then read every third letter, moving clockwise around the square, until all the letters are used.

Start

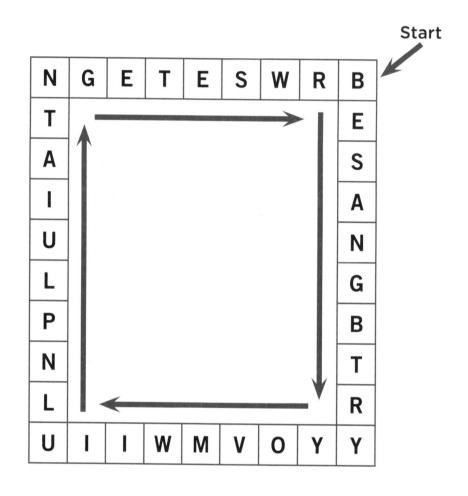

_ _

_ _

BASIC TRAINING

Boxes connected by lines contain the same letter. Some letters are given; others have to be guessed. Fill in all the boxes to reveal a list of items with a connection. Do you know what the connection is?

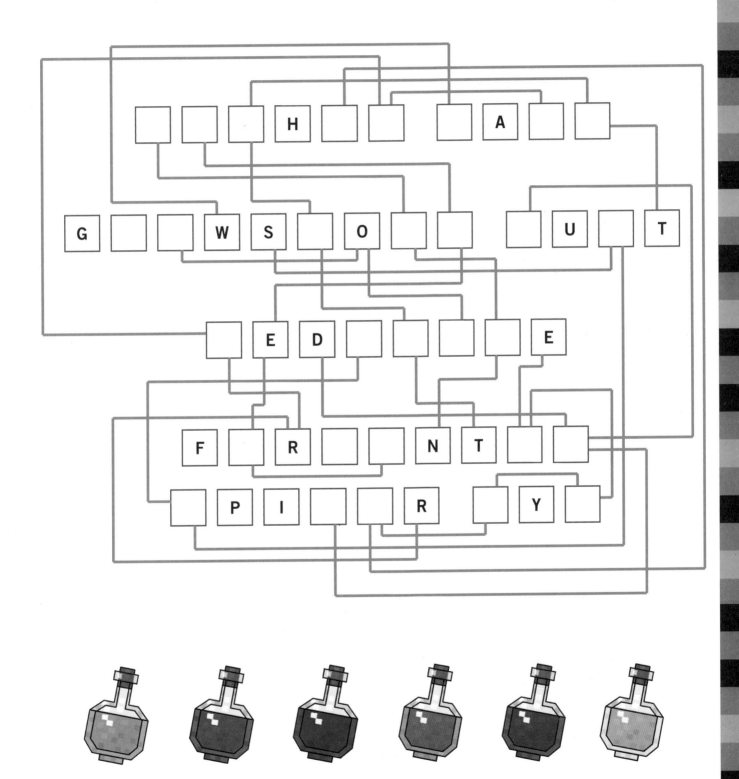

YOU CAN DRAW IT: VILLAGERS

Use the grid to copy the picture. Examine each small square in the top grid, then transfer those lines to the corresponding square in the bottom grid.

THE SHAPE OF THINGS TO COME

Find the six puzzle pieces that fit the shapes in the rectangle. Watch out! Pieces might be rotated or flipped and not all of them will be used. Write the letters of the correct pieces on the spaces below to answer the question:

What mob helps keep creepers away?

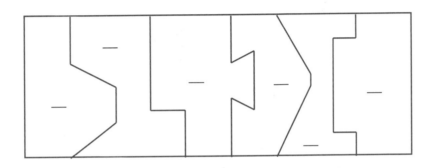

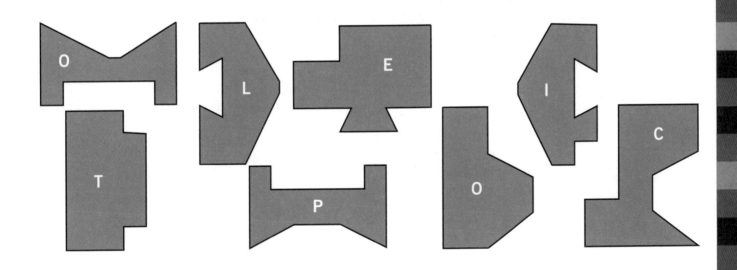

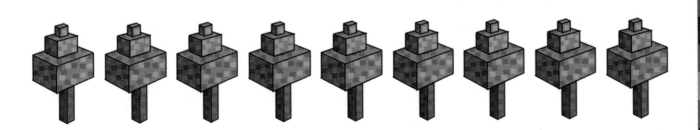

WHEN PIGS HIDE

This pigsty contains thirteen hidden pigs. Can you find them all?

MINER'S BLOCK

Find and circle the names of eight gems in the wordfind below. They might be forward, backward, up, down, or diagonal. Write unused letters on the spaces, in order from top to bottom and left to right, to uncover a tip for mining.

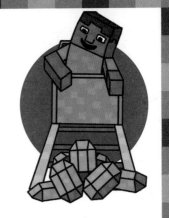

Hint: Circle individual letters instead of the whole word at once. The first one has been done for you.

~~COAL~~	EMERALD	IRON	NETHER QUARTZ
DIAMOND	GOLD	LAPIS LAZULI	REDSTONE

```
R  D  D  I  Ⓛ  G  A  D  R  O  U  N
E  I  L  U  Z  Ⓐ  L  S  I  P  A  L
D  D  O  D  I  A  Ⓞ  A  M  O  N  I
S  D  G  O  R  R  E  Ⓒ  S  O  R  D
T  I  A  E  M  D  I  A  M  O  N  D
O  O  M  N  D  S  D  O  N  N  T  F
N  E  T  H  E  R  Q  U  A  R  T  Z
E  A  L  L  I  N  T  O  L  A  V  A
```

___ ___ ___   ___ ___ ___ ___   ___ ___ ___ ___ ___   ___ ___

___ ___ ___ ___ ___ ___ ___ ___ ,

___ ___ ___ ___ ___ ___ ___ ___ ___ .

TRUE OR FALSE?

Find your way through this maze from Start to Finish. It will be easier if you answer the questions correctly!

Start

FALSE

TRUE

ARROWS WILL CAUSE FIRE DAMAGE IF SHOT THROUGH LAVA

YOU CANNOT FISH UNDER WATER

FALSE

TRUE

ZOMBIE PIGMEN ARE NOT AFFECTED BY LAVA OR FIRE

TRUE

FALSE

WOOD IS MORE EFFICIENT AS FUEL THAN CHARCOAL IS

TRUE

FALSE

Finish

STEVE SAYS: JOKE TIME

Reveal the answer to the joke by doing what Steve says—and only what Steve says! Tip: Cross off the one direction below that you shouldn't follow.

	1	2	3	4	5
A	ONE	CRACKS	HEALING	ALL	STRENGTH
B	418	IF	THIRTEEN	WAX	LEAPING
C	ROADS	HISS	ARE	A	BOOM
D	HACKS	THIRTY	INVISIBILITY	ON	7,359,864
E	RATTLE	BLOCKED	MOAN	IT	SWIFTNESS

1. Steve says, "Cross off all numbers in Rows B and D and Column 1."

2. Steve says, "Cross off all potions in Columns in 3 and 5."

3. Steve says, "Cross off words that rhyme with 'axe.'"

4. Cross off words that start or end with vowels.

5. Steve says, "Cross off all Mob sounds in Rows C and E."

6. Steve says, "Cross off words with fewer than three letters in Columns 2 and 4."

7. Steve says, "Write the remaining four words to reveal the answer to the joke."

Why are there no cars in Minecraft?

_____   _____   _____   _____

ON THE PLAYGROUND

Take a good look to find the ten differences between these two pictures.

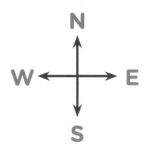

ENCHANTED MAP

This End City map is enchanted. To reveal its contents, you must press all twelve buttons in the right order and land on the F button last. Use the letters and numbers on the buttons to direct you.

Which button must you push first to get to F last?

Hint: 1N means press the button one space north; 2E means move two spaces east. W=west and S=south.

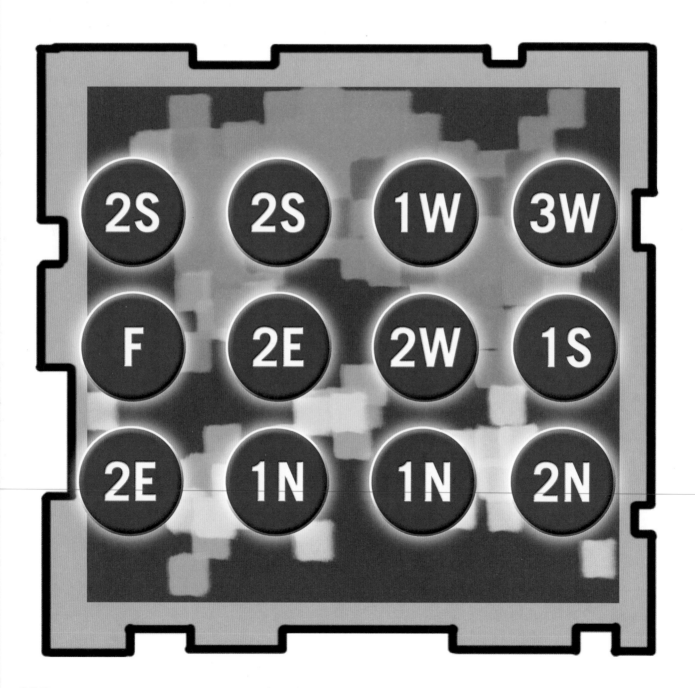

COMMON CODE

Use the key to identify three items that are familiar to Minecrafters. Then use the key to fill in the last set of blank spaces to reveal where all three items are found.

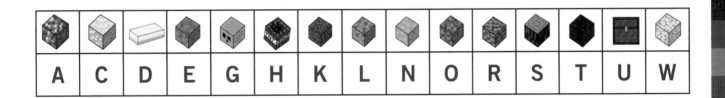

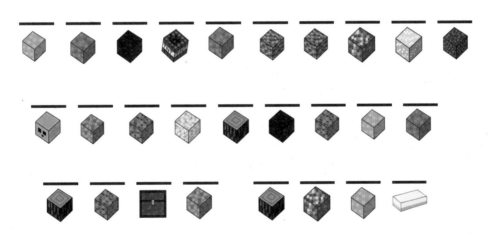

What do the three words above have in common?

They're all found in

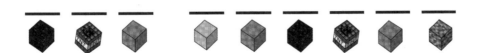

EVERY NOOK AND CRANNY

Draw a line from Start to Stop that passes through every apple once and only once. Your line can go up, down, left, or right, but not diagonally. On your mark, get set, go!

Start

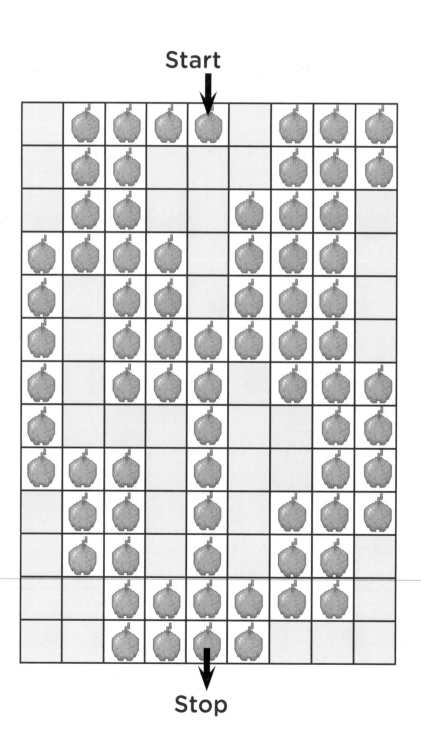

Stop

CIRCLE OF TRUTH: SURVIVAL TIP

Start at the ⬇. Write every third letter on the spaces to reveal a truth about Minecraft.

W E A R   A   P U M P K I N   O N   Y O U R

H E A D ,

A N D   E N D E R M E N   W O N ' T   A T T A C K   Y O U

SKELETON TWINS

Only two of these skeletons are exactly the same. Which two are identical? Circle the twins.

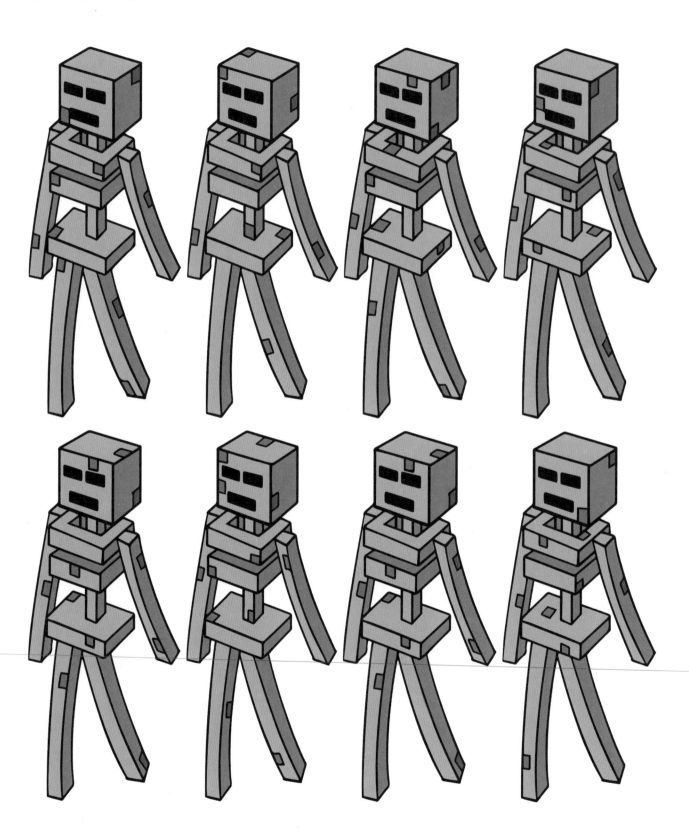

CONNECT THE DOTS: PIT OF PERIL!

Connect the dots to complete this perilous scene.

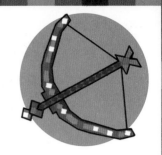

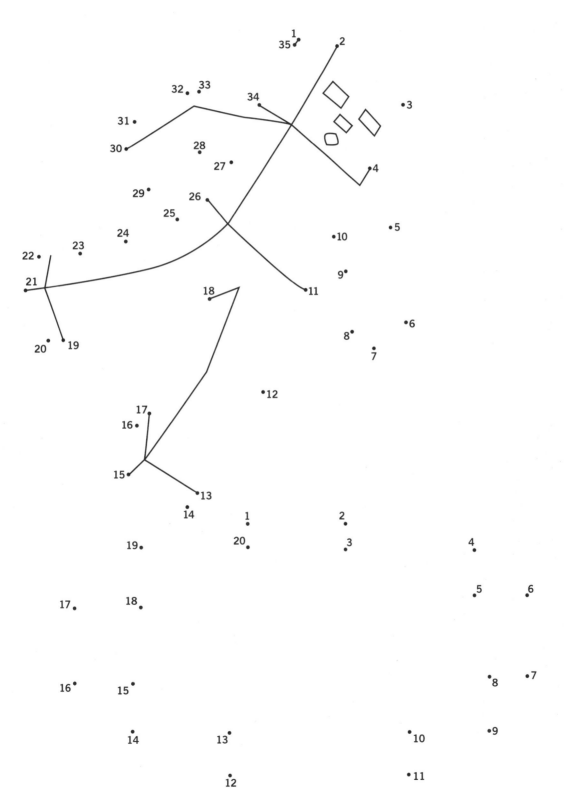

SQUARED UP: BLOCK PARTY

Each of the six blocks in this puzzle can appear only once in each row, each column, and pink rectangle. Use the letter C to represent a clay block, the letter D for a dirt block, and so on. Can you fill every square with the right letter?

 C = Clay   D = Dirt   G = Gravel   I = Ice   O = Obsidian   S = Sand

	I	G	C	O	
O	C			G	I
I		S	D		G
D		C	O		S
C	S			D	O
	D	O	I	S	

HOLD IT!

It's time to discuss a weighty matter. Start with the corner letter, then read every third letter, moving clockwise around the square, and write them in the blank spaces below until you solve the mystery message.

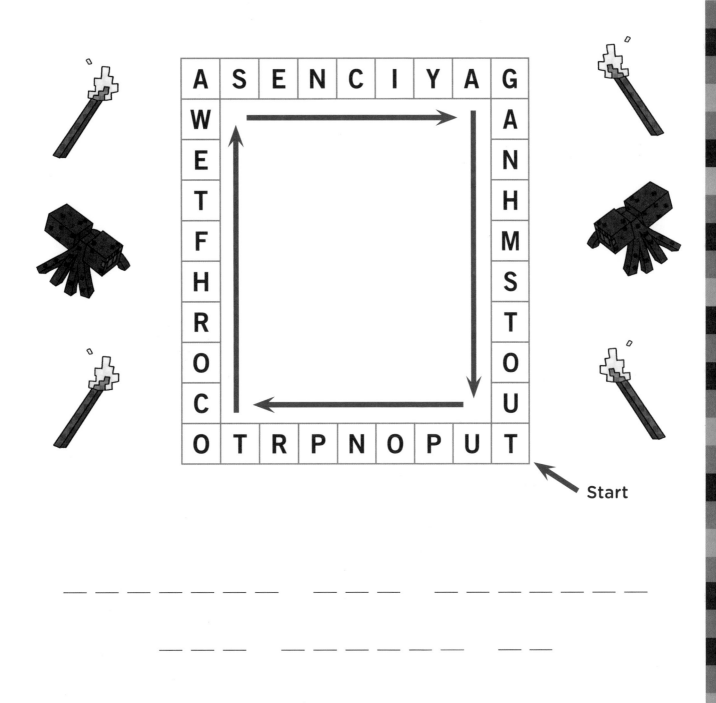

Start

‾ ‾ ‾ ‾ ‾ ‾ ‾ ‾   ‾ ‾ ‾   ‾ ‾ ‾ ‾ ‾ ‾

‾ ‾ ‾   ‾ ‾ ‾ ‾ ‾   ‾ ‾

‾ ‾ ‾ ‾ ‾ ‾

COLLECTING TREASURE

Four treasures are yours for the taking—and you want them all! Find the path that allows you to collect the four treasures between Start and Finish. Heads up! Paths go under and over each other.

Start

Finish

CIRCLE OF TRUTH: FOOD FOR THOUGHT

Start at the ▼.

Write every third letter on the spaces to reveal a Minecrafting secret.

E _ _ _ _ _   _ _ _ _ _ _ _ _ _ _

_ _ _ _ _ _   _ _ _ _ _ _ _ _ _ ,

_ _ _ _ _ _ ,   _ _ _   _ _ _ _ _ _

YOU CAN DRAW IT: IRON GOLEM

Use the grid to copy the picture. Examine the lines in each small square in the grid at the left, then transfer those lines to the corresponding square in the grid on the right.

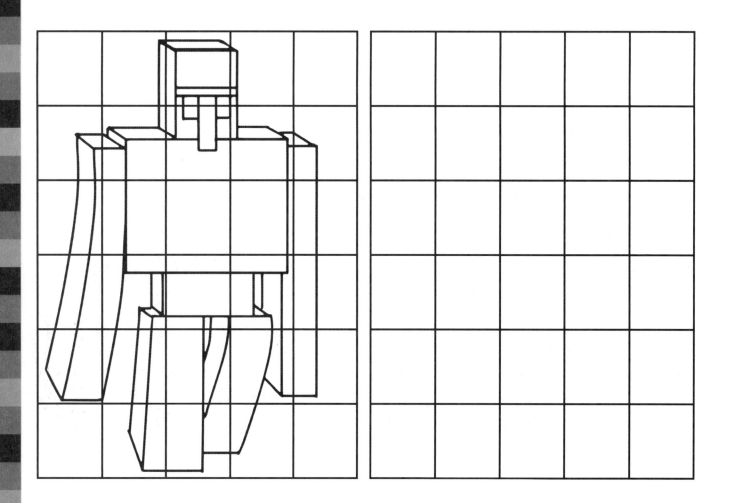

TIP FOR ENDING ENDERMEN

Step 1: Find the ten puzzle pieces that fit the shapes in the rectangle. Watch out! Pieces might be rotated or flipped. Write the letters of the correct pieces on the spaces. Not all pieces are used below.

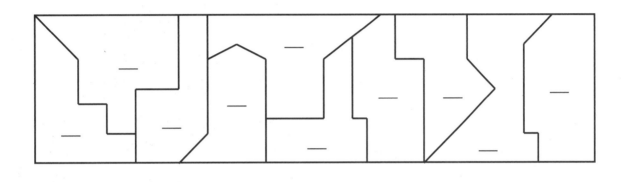

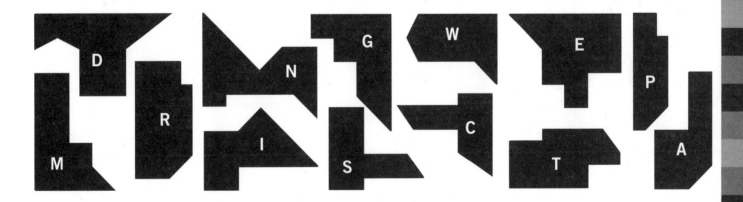

Step 2: Write the letters from the spaces above in the boxes that have the same numbers to reveal something that can help you destroy Endermen.

6	7	3	9	5

8	9

4	3	7	2	10

211

WORD FARM

The words bat, cow, pig, sheep, spider, squid, chicken, donkey, mule, polar bear, rabbit, ocelot, *and* wolf *are hiding on this farm. How many words can you spot?*

CONNECT THE DOTS: FARM LIFE

Connect the dots to to see what's happening on the Minecrafter's farm.

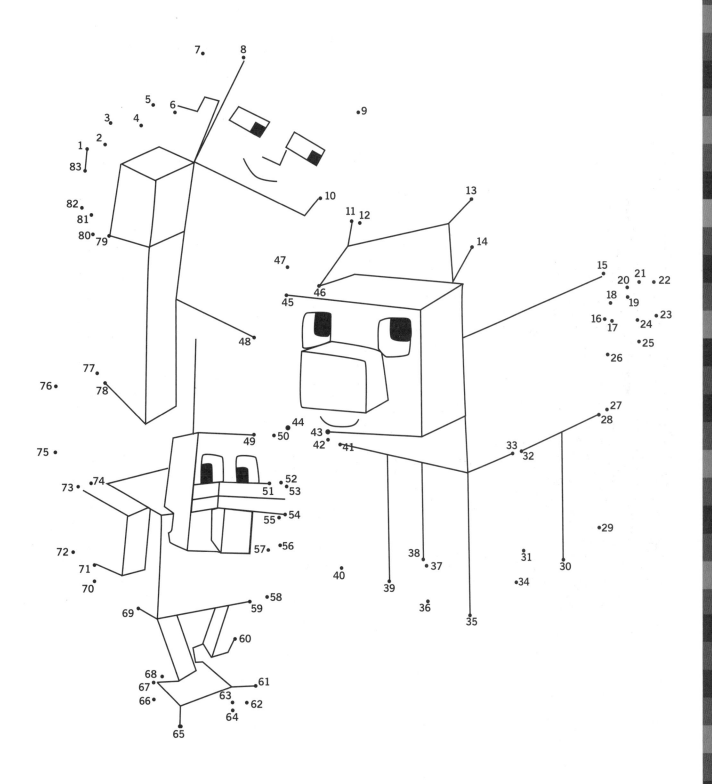

HUNT FOR ENCHANTMENTS

Find and circle the names of fifteen enchantments in the wordfind below. They might be forward, backward, up, down, or diagonal. Write unused letters on the blank spaces, in order from *left to right and top to bottom*, to discover a fun fact about enchantments.

Hint: Circle individual letters instead of whole words. We've found one to get you started.

```
H  O  O  K  C  A  B  K  C  O  N  K
E  F  F  I  C  I  E  N  C  Y  K  M
P  O  I  S  M  I  T  E  R  S  I  G
R  E  F  R  I  S  N  H  H  W  N  N
O  E  G  I  E  U  T  A  H  I  F  I
T  M  T  N  T  A  R  H  K  E  I  D
E  A  P  R  I  P  S  A  L  P  N  N
C  L  O  O  N  T  E  P  U  U  I  E
T  F  R  E  W  R  O  E  E  N  T  M
I  E  S  N  B  E  C  O  H  C  Y  A
O  S  N  N  T  M  R  E  L  H  T  N
N  T  U  S  I  L  K  T  O  U  C  H
```

EFFICIENCY
FIRE ASPECT
FLAME
FORTUNE
INFINITY
KNOCKBACK
~~LOOTING~~
MENDING
POWER
PROTECTION
PUNCH
SHARPNESS
SILK TOUCH
SMITE
UNBREAKING

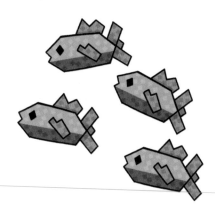

_ _ _ _   _ _ _ _   _ _ _ _   _ _ _ _

_ _ _   _ _ _ _   _ _ _ _ _ _ _ _ _

214

ROTTEN LUCK

Take your chances with this dangerous maze and avoid food poisoning at all costs. Choose a path from the Start box. There's only one lucky path that leads to a quiet corner and a delicious cookie. The rest lead to the dreaded rotten flesh! Good luck!

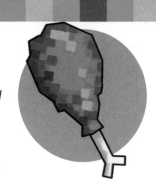

Start

YOU WIN!

BAD LUCK AHEAD!

TURN BACK!

DANGER

MULTIPLAYER MISMATCH

These two pictures are nearly identical, except for ten little differences.
How many of these differences can you find?

TWIN MOBS

Only two of these villagers are exactly the same.
Which two are identical?

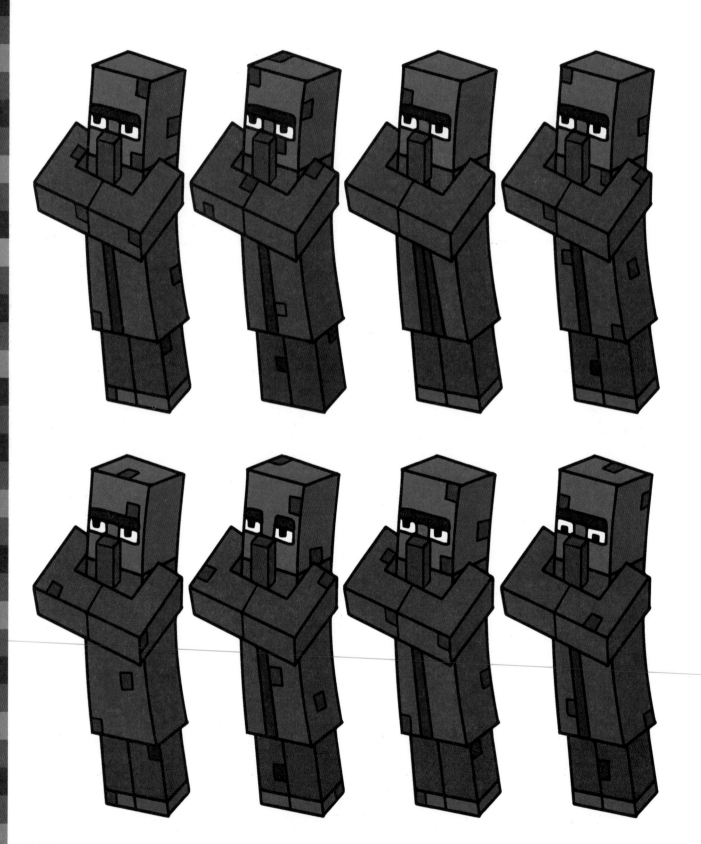

CONNECT THE DOTS: OUR HERO

Connect the dots and find out who always saves the day.

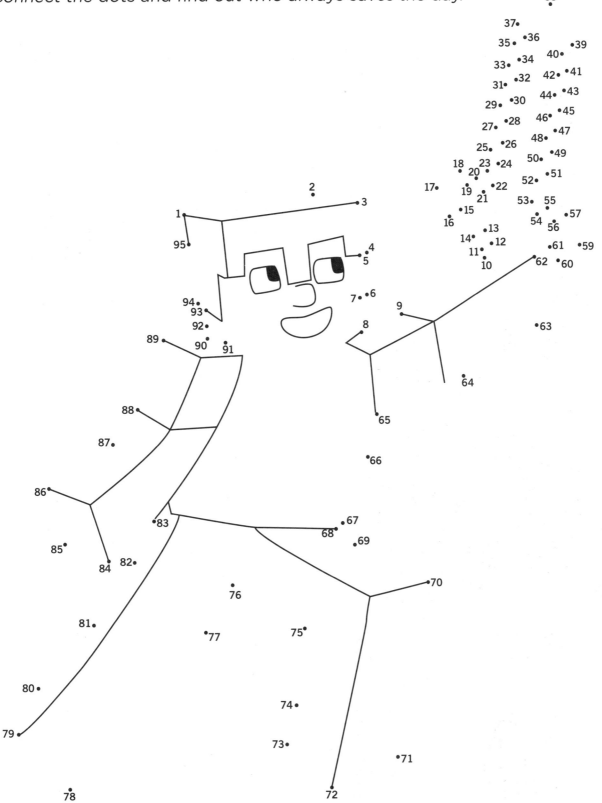

ANSWER KEY

PAGE 154 STEVE SAYS...

CREEPERS WERE THE RESULT OF A CODING MISTAKE

(What was supposed to be a pig wound up with extra-long legs, and the result turned into a creeper.)

PAGE 155 THE MIRROR'S IMAGE

ENDERMEN WERE CALLED "FARLANDERS" BEFORE THE END WAS CREATED

PAGE 156 CITY SLICKER

PAGE 158 TAKE A GUESS

EXIT, CORN, PINE, SEEP

EXPERIENCE POINTS

PAGE 159 ENCHANTED CHEST

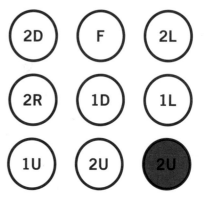

The red button is the first one pressed.

PAGE 160 SEE AND SOLVE

```
      L A V A
  F   R
  R   R
  I   R
  S H O V E L       I
  H     W     E     N
              L     G
        C A R R O T
        L     Y     T
        A     T
        Y     A
```

THEY FIRE EVERYONE

PAGE 161 HOME SWEET BIOME

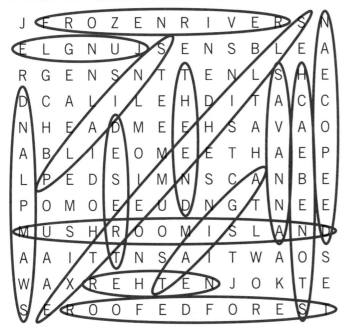

PAGE 162 CREEPER TWINS

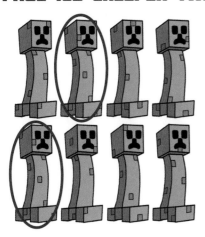

PAGE 163 CIRCLE OF TRUTH: CRAFTING CLUE

DIAMOND MAKES THE STRONGEST TOOLS

PAGE 164 MOB SCENE

1. S E A R C H
2. E X P E R T
3. A P P L E S
4. P L A Y E R
5. O U T P U T
6. S A D D L E
7. S P I D E R
8. N O I S E
9. E G G

EXPLODING CREEPERS

PAGE 165 SQUARED UP: MOBS IN EVERY QUARTER

G	C	S	B
B	S	G	C
C	G	B	S
S	B	C	G

PAGE 166 WATCHTOWER QUEST

PAGE 167
A CURE FOR WHAT AILS YOU

DRINKING A BUCKET OF MILK CURES POISONING

PAGE 169 PIECE IT TOGETHER

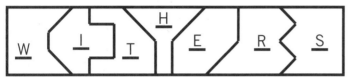

W I T H E R S

PAGE 170   PICK, THE RIGHT TOOL!

PAGE 171   TOOL CHEST

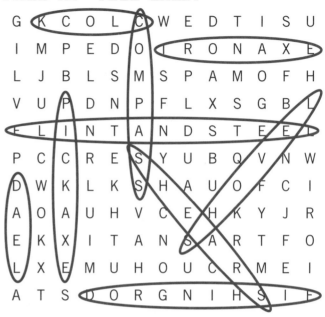

PAGE 172   FIND THE PORTAL

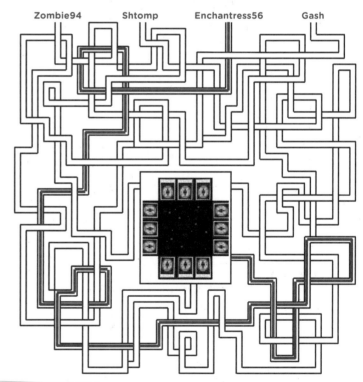

Enchantress56 finds the portal.

PAGE 173
CROSSWORD CLUE FINDER

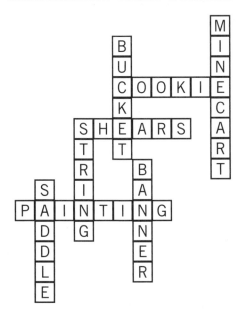

PAGE 177 SURVIVAL MAZE

PAGE 174–175 SEE THE SEA

PAGE 178 BLOCKED!

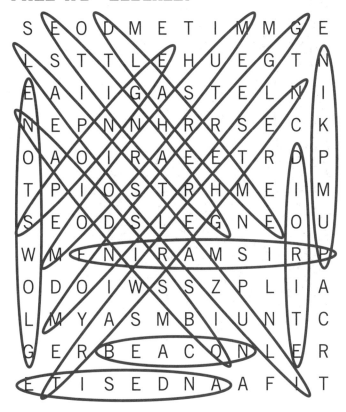

PAGE 176
POWER PLAY: MYSTERY WORD

REDSTONE

PAGE 179
CONNECT THE DOTS: HOSTILE MOB

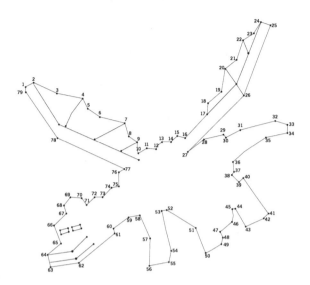

PAGE 180   MIXED UP

GRIN, NOON, PIG, TILE
LINGERING POTION

PAGE 181   A SMALL PROBLEM

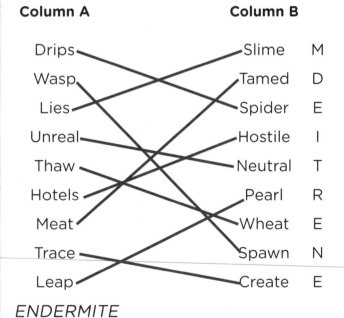

Column A

Drips
Wasp
Lies
Unreal
Thaw
Hotels
Meat
Trace
Leap

Column B

Slime — M
Tamed — D
Spider — E
Hostile — I
Neutral — T
Pearl — R
Wheat — E
Spawn — N
Create — E

ENDERMITE

PAGE 182   CRACK THE CODE

IT WAS A POUND CAKE

PAGE 183   ALPHA CODE

| B | E | C | A | U | S | E | | I | T |

C F D B V T F   J U
D G E C W U G   K V

R S Z Q S D C

| S | T | A | R | T | E | D |

T U B S U F E

Y R   R F C   C L B
Z S   S G D   D M C

| A | T | | T | H | E | | E | N | D |

PAGE 184
GRAB AND GO CHALLENGE

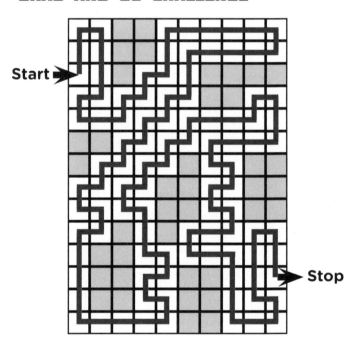

Start ➤

Stop

224

PAGE 185　WORD MINE

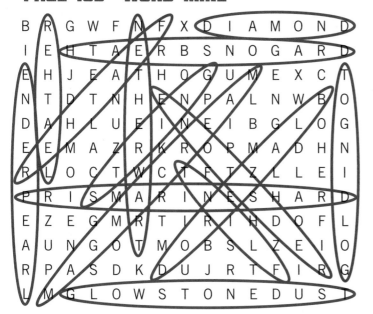

```
B R G W F N F X D I A M O N D
I E H T A E R B S N O G A R D
E H J E A T H O G U M E X C T
N T D T N H E N P A L N W B O
D A H L U E I N E I B G L O G
E E M A Z R K R O P M A D H N
R L O C T W C F T Z L L E I I
P R I S M A R I N E S H A R D
E Z E G M R T I R I H D O F L
A U N G O T M O B S L Z E I O
R P A S D K D U J R T F I R G
L M G L O W S T O N E D U S T
```

PAGE 186 CIRCLE OF TRUTH: FUN FACT

YOU CAN'T OPEN A CHEST IF A CAT SITS ON IT

PAGE 187　ZOMBIE TWINS

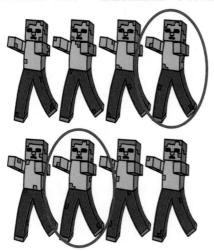

PAGE 188　CAN YOU DIG IT?

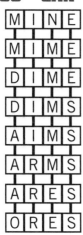

M	I	N	E
M	I	M	E
D	I	M	E
D	I	M	S
A	I	M	S
A	R	M	S
A	R	E	S
O	R	E	S

PAGE 189
SQUARED UP: FARM MOBS

S	H	C	P
P	C	H	S
C	P	S	H
H	S	P	C

PAGE 190
GROW WITH THE FLOW

BABY VILLAGERS GROW UP IN TWENTY MINUTES

You start in the top right corner.

PAGE 191
BASIC TRAINING

NETHER WART
GLOWSTONE DUST
REDSTONE
FERMENTED SPIDER EYE
These are the base brewing ingredients.

PAGE 193
THE SHAPE OF THINGS TO COME

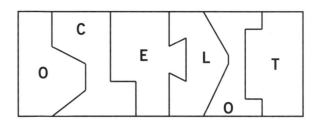

PAGE 194 WHEN PIGS HIDE

PAGE 195 MINER'S BLOCK

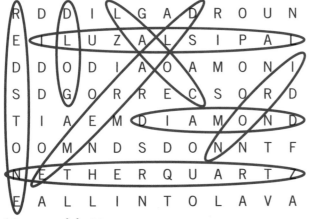

Unused letters:

*DIG AROUND DIAMOND ORE
SO DIAMONDS DON'T FALL
INTO LAVA*

PAGE 196 TRUE OR FALSE?

Start

FALSE

TRUE · Arrows will cause fire damage if shot through lava

You cannot fish under water · FALSE

TRUE

Zombie pigmen are not affected by lava or fire · FALSE

TRUE

Wood is more efficient as fuel than charcoal · TRUE

FALSE

Finish

PAGE 197 STEVE SAYS: JOKE TIME

ALL ROADS ARE BLOCKED

PAGE 198 ON THE PLAYGROUND

PAGE 200 ENCHANTED MAP

(2S) (2S) (1W) (3W)

(F) (2E) (2W) (1S)

(2E) (1N) (1N) (2N)

The red button is the first one pressed.

PAGE 201 COMMON CODE

NETHERRACK, GLOWSTONE, SOUL SAND
These things are found only in the Nether

PAGE 202 EVERY NOOK AND CRANNY

Start

Stop

PAGE 203
CIRCLE OF TRUTH: SURVIVAL TIP

*WEAR A PUMPKIN ON YOUR
HEAD AND ENDERMEN WON'T
GET ANGRY WITH YOU*

PAGE 204   SKELETON TWINS

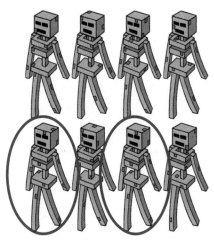

PAGE 205
CONNECT THE DOTS: PIT OF PERIL

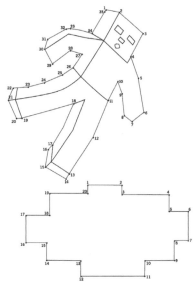

PAGE 206
SQUARED UP: BLOCK PARTY

S	I	G	C	O	D
O	C	D	S	G	I
I	O	S	D	C	G
D	G	C	O	I	S
C	S	I	G	D	O
G	D	O	I	S	C

PAGE 207   HOLD IT!

*TORCHES CAN SUPPORT ANY
AMOUNT OF WEIGHT*

PAGE 208 COLLECTING TREASURE

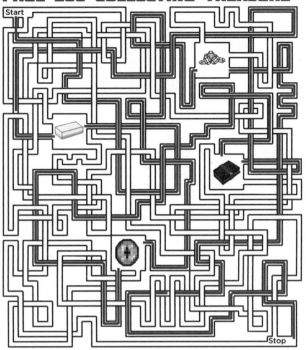

PAGE 209
CIRCLE OF TRUTH:
FOOD FOR THOUGHT

*EATING PUFFERFISH CAUSES
POISONING, HUNGER, AND NAUSEA*

PAGE 211
TIP FOR ENDING ENDERMEN

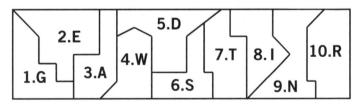

STAND IN WATER

PAGE 212
WORD FARM

PAGE 213
CONNECT THE DOTS: FARM LIFE

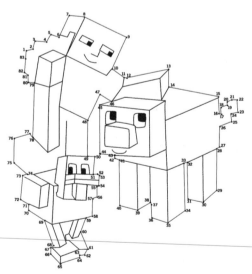

PAGE 214
HUNT FOR ENCHANTMENTS

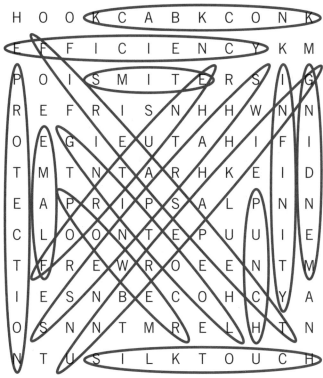

Unused letters:

HOOK MORE FISH WITH THE LURE ENCHANTMENT

PAGE 215
ROTTEN LUCK

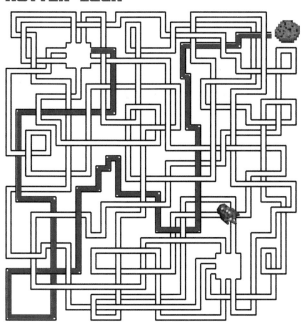

PAGE 216 MULTIPLAYER MISMATCH

PAGE 218 TWIN MOBS

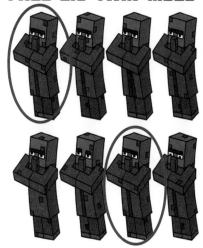

PAGE 219
CONNECT THE DOTS: OUR HERO

LANGUAGE ARTS FOR
MINECRAFTERS

Printing

Practice

A 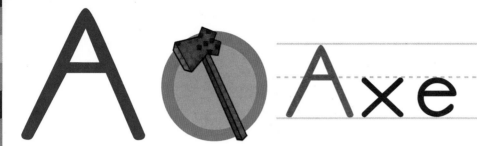 Axe

A

a   axe

1a2   a   a   a   a

B Bed

B B B B B B

b

bed

b b b b

C  Creeper

C C C C C C

C  creeper

C¹ c c c c c

D Dog

D

d

dog

d   d   d   d   d

E  Enderman

E E E E E

e  enderman

e 1   e   e   e   e

F

Fish

F

2 → 1 ↓ 3 →

F   F   F   F   F

f   fish

G 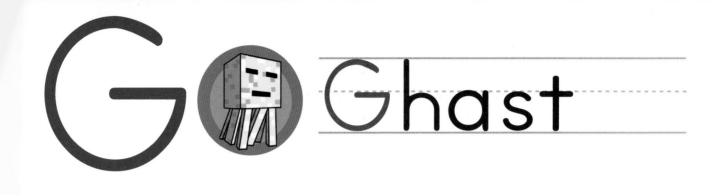 Ghast

g  ghast

¹g² g g g g

H

Helmet

H

h

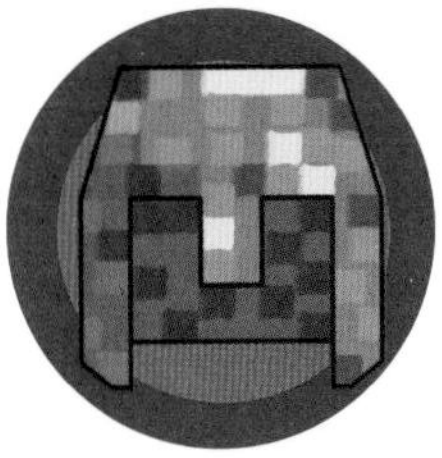

helmet

h h h h h

I

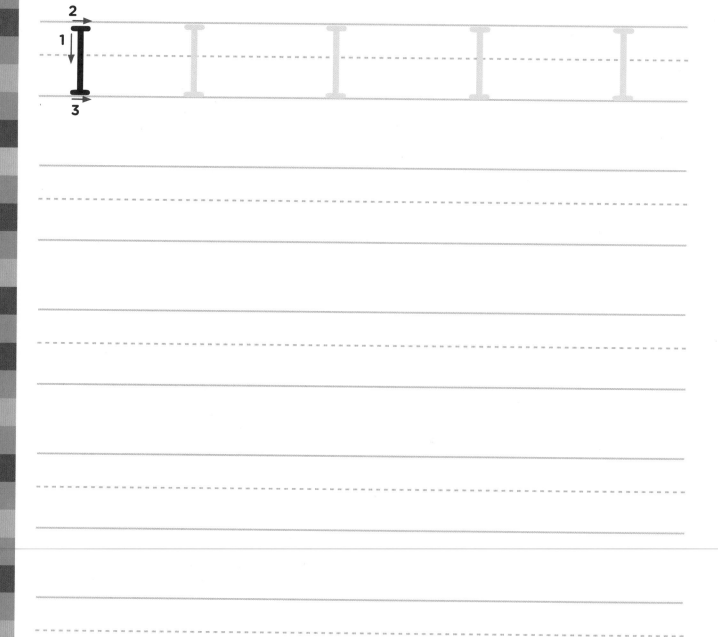

Ice

i

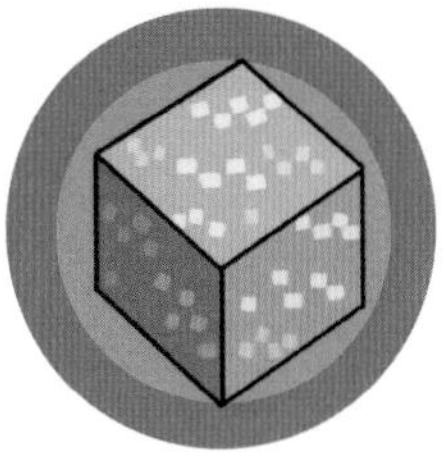

ice

i i i i i

J

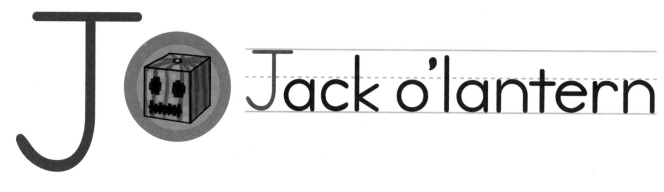

Jack o'lantern

2 →
1 ↓

J   J   J   J   J

j

jack o'lantern

j

K

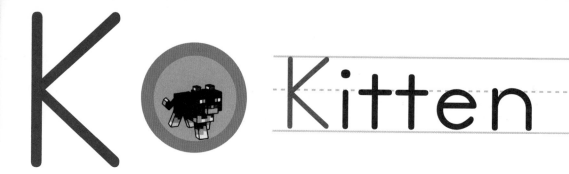 Kitten

k  kitten

k k k k

L

Lava

l

lava

1

M  Map

M M M M M M

m  map

m m m m m m

N  Night

N N N N N N

n  night

n

Orb

1

orb

P

Potion

P

p potion

p p p p p

Q Quick

Q
1
2

q  quick

1 2 q   q   q   q   q   q

R

Railway

r  railway

S

Skeleton

S s s s s

S  skeleton

S¹

S S S S S

T

Torch

t

torch

U

U Unpack

U

u  unpack

u u u u

V  Villager

V

V  villager

W 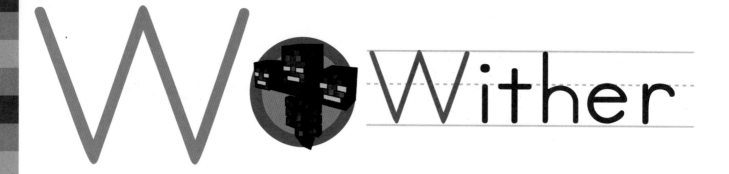 Wither

W  wither

1 2 3 4
W   W   W   W   W

X X-ray mod

X X X X X

X 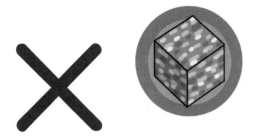 x-ray mod

X

Yellow

Y

y  yellow

1 2 y y y y y

Z  Zombie

Z

Z

zombie

1 →
2 ↙ Z 3 →

Z   Z   Z   Z

THE ALPHABET

Trace all of the alphabet letters to review what you learned.

A B C D E

F G H I J

K L M N O

P Q R S T

U V W X Y Z

a b c d e

f g h i j

k l m n o

p q r s t

u v w x y z

NAME PRACTICE

Practice writing your name on the lines below.

WORD PRACTICE

Now practice writing the names of these hostile mobs.

 creeper

 zombie

 wither

 skeleton

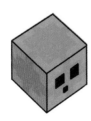 slime

WORD PRACTICE

Practice writing the names of these passive and neutral mobs.

ocelot

squid

wolf

spider

villager

Steve mined diamonds and crafted these items. Practice writing the item names.

 sword

 pickaxe

 shovel

Practice writing the name of Alex's enchanted weapon.

bow and arrow

SENTENCE PRACTICE

Copy the Minecrafting sentences below.

Iron golems protect villagers.

Zombies drop rotten flesh.

Ghasts shoot fireballs.

Diamond weapons are strong.

Endermen can teleport.

Creepers hate cats.

Withers are deadly.

LANGUAGE ARTS FOR MINECRAFTERS

READING

SHORT A

*Draw a line to connect the picture with the **short a** word.*

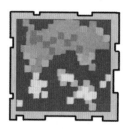

apple

map

bat

axe

cat

SHORT A

Finish each sentence with one of these **short a** words.

apple   map   bat   axe   cat

1. I eat a golden _____ so I can get hunger points.

2. The _____ flies around the cave.

3. The _____ helps me find my way around.

4. My black _____ likes to eat fish.

5. I dig and dig with my _____ .

LONG A

*Draw a line to connect the picture with the **long a** word.*

cake

play

blaze

lay

race

LONG A

*Finish each sentence with one of these **long a** words.*

cake   play   blaze   lay   race

1. Steve made a _____ for Alex's birthday.

2. She is attacked by the yellow _____ .

3. Steve will _____ back to safety.

4. The chicken will _____ five eggs.

5. Steve likes to _____ and have fun.

SHORT E

*Draw a line to connect the picture with the **short e** word.*

Enderman

skeleton

egg

bed

red

SHORT E

*Finish each sentence with one of these **short e** words.*

Enderman   skeleton   egg   bed   red

1. The purple _____ has a shulker inside.

2. The block is _____.

3. Steve will battle the bony _____.

4. You can build a _____ with wood.

5. The tall, black _____ is afraid of water.

LONG E

*Draw a line to connect the picture with the **long e** word.*

beef

creeper

tree

wheat

she

LONG E

*Finish each sentence with one of these **long e** words.*

beef   creeper   tree   wheat   she

1. Steve feeds bunches of _____ to the horse.

2. Destroy a cow and you can collect raw _____.

3. Don't get too close to a _____ when

   it explodes.

4. Plant saplings if you want a _____ to grow.

5. Alex wears her armor when _____ wants to win a battle.

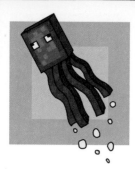

SHORT I

*Draw a line to connect the picture with the **short i** word.*

fish

pickaxe

squid

Wither

pigman

SHORT I

*Finish each sentence with one of these **short i** words.*

fish   pickaxe   squid   **Wither**   **pigman**

1. A zombie _____ spawns when lightning strikes near a pig.

2. A diamond _____ is a very good tool for mining.

3. The black _____ swims in the water and drops ink.

4. The _____ has three heads!

5. When I get hungry, I can try to catch a _____ .

LONG I

*Draw a line to connect the picture with the **long i** word.*

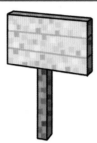

ice block

iron golem

night

ride

sign

LONG I

*Finish each sentence with one of these **long i** words.*

ice blocks   iron golem   night   ride   sign

1. You can break _____ in the Ice

    Plains Biome.

2. The _____ is a neutral mob that

    protects villages.

3. You can write what you want on the wooden _____ .

4. Zombies and other scary mobs come out at _____ .

5. Jump in and _____ in a minecart!

SHORT O

*Draw a line to connect the picture with the **short o** word.*

 cobweb

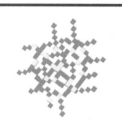 ocelot

 block

 zombie

 donkey

SHORT O

*Finish each sentence with one of these **short o** words.*

cobwebs   ocelot   blocks   zombie   donkey

1. I feed the _____ some fish to tame it.

2. I build a shelter with ten granite _____ .

3. The moaning _____ only attacks at night.

4. There are _____ hanging in the spider's cave.

5. A _____ looks a lot like a horse.

grow

bone

arrow

potion

explosive

LONG O

*Finish each sentence with one of these **long o** words.*

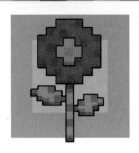

grow   bone   potion   arrow   explosive

1. The flower will _____ in the garden.

2. Feed the wolf a _____ and it will be your pet.

3. Use a _____ of Swiftness to escape the creeper.

4. The skeleton shoots an _____ at Steve.

5. Blocks of TNT are great for setting _____ traps.

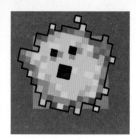

SHORT U

*Draw a line to connect the picture with the **short u** word.*

pufferfish

mushroom

hunger bar

bucket

bunny

SHORT U

*Finish each sentence with one of these **short u** words.*

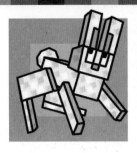

mushrooms   **pufferfish**   **hunger bar**   **bucket**   **bunny**

1. The white _____ hops over to Steve.

2. A _____ full of water can scare Endermen away.

3. The bony _____ tells a player if they need to eat.

4. I catch a _____ with my fishing rod.

5. Alex picks the red _____ to make stew.

LONG U

*Draw a line to connect the picture with the **long u** word.*

huge

blue

cube

fruit

suit

LONG U

*Finish each sentence with one of these **long u** words.*

blue   huge   cube   fruit   suit

1. The player's bucket is _____ .

2. Each block in the game is shaped like a _____ .

3. Alex puts on a _____ of armor to battle the Ender Dragon.

4. An apple is a kind of _____ .

5. The giant zombie looks _____ next to the villager.

SENTENCES

A **sentence** is a group of words that tells a complete thought. All sentences begin with a **capital letter**. A statement ends with a **period**. A sentence includes a **noun**, a **verb**, and sometimes an **adjective**.

A **noun** is a person, place, or thing.

A **verb** is an action word.

An **adjective** is a description word.

1. Draw a triangle around the **capital letter** that begins the sentence.

2. Circle the **noun** (there may be more than one).

3. Underline the **verb**.

4. Draw a rectangle around the **adjective**.

5. Draw a square around the **period** that ends the sentence.

1. The green creepers dance.

2. The player crafts an iron sword.

3. Alex fills the open chest.

4. The baby zombie rides a chicken.

5. The skeleton shoots a sharp arrow.

THE PIG

Read about the Minecraft pig.
Then write **true** or **false** for the statements on the next page.

This is a pig. Pigs spawn on grass blocks.

Pigs roam the Overworld. They do not like

water. Baby pigs are called piglets. Piglets

grow into pigs in twenty minutes.

1. Pigs spawn on sandstone. _____

2. Pigs live in the Overworld. _____

3. Pigs like water. _____

4. A piglet is an adult pig. _____

5. Piglets grow into pigs in
   twenty minutes. _____

THIS IS THE WOLF

Read about the wolf.
Then connect the phrases in the left column with the correct answers in the right column.

This is a wolf. The wolf has gray fur. He can be wild, mean, or tame. A wild wolf has black eyes. A mean wolf has red eyes. A tame wolf has a red collar. The wolf lives in a pack. A wolf spawns in packs of four.

The wolf's fur is ...   **black eyes**

A wild wolf has ....   **a red collar**

A mean wolf has ....   **gray**

A tame wolf has ....   **red eyes**

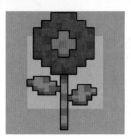

MEET THE COW

Read about the cow.
Then answer the questions on the next page.

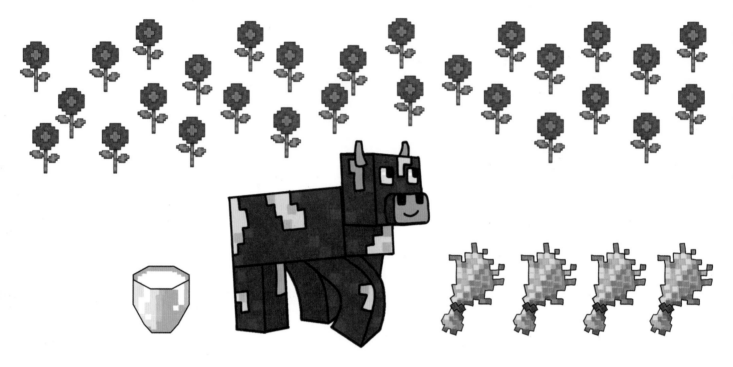

This is a cow. The cow has gray spots.

Cows walk slowly. Cows will follow wheat.

If you have a bucket, you can milk a cow.

1. What color are the cow's spots?

The cow's spots are _____ .

2. How do cows walk?

Cows walk _____ .

3. What does a cow follow?

A cow follows _____ .

4. What do you need to milk a cow?

You need a _____ to milk a cow.

SADDLE UP!

Read about the horse.
Then use the words to fill in the blanks on the next page.

Horses come in seven colors. Some horses

have spots. This horse is eating carrots.

He likes carrots because they are crunchy.

A saddle lets you ride the horse. It takes

a long time to tame a horse. The horse is

tame when it shows hearts. Some horses

can jump high.

Choose from the words below to fill in the blanks.

black	tasty	crunchy
brown	seven	farms
flowers	saddle	hearts

1. The horse comes in _____ colors.

2. The horse likes eating carrots because they are

   _____

   _____ .

3. A _____ lets you ride the horse.

4. When a horse is tame, it shows _____ .

WATCH OUT FOR ZOMBIES!

Read about zombies. Then answer the questions on the next page.

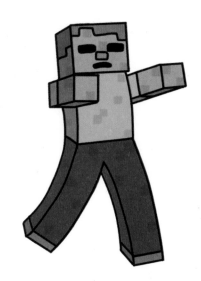

This is a zombie. Zombies are slow, so it is easy to run away from them. Their groaning sounds let you know they are nearby. Sunlight can kill a zombie. Zombies can call other zombies to help them fight. If a zombie attacks you, it can turn you into a zombie too.

1. Zombies are

☐ Fast   ☐ Slow   ☐ Quiet

2. What kind of sounds do zombies make?

☐ Moaning   ☐ Screaming   ☐ Groaning

3. What can kill a zombie?

☐ Sunlight   ☐ Darkness   ☐ Other zombies

4. Who can zombies call to help them fight?

☐ Wolves   ☐ Other zombies   ☐ Dragons

5. If a zombie attacks you, it can turn you into a

☐ Robot   ☐ Zombie   ☐ Zombie robot

CREEPY CREEPERS

Read about creepers.
Then finish the statements on the next page.

Creepers are green and very quiet. They like to hide in caves. Creepers will sneak up on you and then explode. This will harm anything near the blast. They are afraid of cats, so keep a cat with you at all times. Climbing a ladder to escape a creeper will not work. It's better to hide behind closed doors.

1. Creepers can sneak up on you because they are

_____

_____ .

2. Creepers might be hiding in a _____ .

3. If they _____ , you could be harmed.

4. Creepers have a fear of _____ .

5. Creepers can't open doors, but they can climb

_____

_____ .

THE ENDER DRAGON

Read about the Ender Dragon.
Then fill in the blanks on the next page.

The Ender Dragon is a boss mob. It lives in the End. It flies in circles in the sky. It can charge at players. It likes to perch on the tallest block. It can send out purple balls of fire. Some Ender Dragons drop an egg when destroyed.

1. The Ender Dragon is a _____ mob.

2. The dragon lives in the _____ .

3. The dragon flies in _____ in the sky.

4. The balls of fire are _____ .

5. To get an egg from an Ender Dragon, you have to _____ it.

MINECRAFT BOATS, NEW AND IMPROVED

Read about Minecrafters' boats.
Then answer the questions on the next page.

The boats in the new version of the game are much better than the boats in the old version. The new boats are stronger and don't break apart so easily. They also come with paddles. The boats in the new version go faster than the boats in the old version. Plus, the new boats can carry two people. They are a new great way to move around.

What is the main idea of this text?

Give three details that support the main idea.

1.

2.

3.

THE GHAST

Read about ghasts.
Then circle the correct answer to the questions on the next page.

The ghast was floating in the Nether world. Its eyes and mouth were closed. Its legs swayed gently. The ghast was sad because it could not leave the Nether world. Then it sensed someone was nearby. It opened its black mouth and eyes. It made high-pitched screams. The ghast shot its fireballs at the enemy, who hid behind a wall. The ghast floated and dropped more fireballs. An arrow flew by its legs. Then more arrows flew by even closer. The fight was on!

1. The ghast:

A. Moved quickly   B. Floated   C. Stayed in one place

2. The ghast was:

A. Happy   B. Excited   C. Sad

3. The ghast's mouth and eyes are:

A. White   B. Black   C. Red

4. The ghast shot:

A. Fireballs   B. Arrows   C. Screams

5. The arrow almost hit the ghast's:

A. Head   B. Mouth   C. Legs

ALL ABOUT POTIONS

Read about potions.
Then fill out the chart on the next page.

Potions give you special powers. To make potions, you must get certain things from the Nether. You also need to have a brewing stand. Almost all potions start with a base potion. Some potions are green, blue, purple, red, yellow, or orange. A green potion lets you jump high. A blue potion lets you see at night. A purple potion brings you back to health. A red potion makes you stronger. A yellow potion gives you a health boost. An orange potion protects you from fire.

Potion Colors and Their Effects

COLOR	EFFECT
Green	
Blue	
Purple	
Red	
Yellow	
Orange	

STEVE'S BIRTHDAY

Read the story about Steve's birthday.
Then answer the questions on the next page.

Today is Steve's birthday, and he turns nine. He is very excited to have a party. He hopes he gets a new video game for a present. His friends will come over at four o'clock for cake and ice cream. But the cake looks so good. Steve thinks it will be okay if he just tries a small piece. Yum! It is so tasty! Steve thinks he will take another slice. He can smooth the frosting over what he has eaten and no one will notice. The frosting is so good, too! Maybe just another little piece. Uh oh! The cake is almost gone now. Steve hears his mom in the hall.

"Steve!" she yells. "You ate all the cake! I told you to leave the cake alone. You will have to call your friends and tell them the party is cancelled!"

1. What is the cause of the mother's anger?

_____

_____

_____

_____

_____

_____

2. What is the effect of the mother's anger?

_____

_____

_____

_____

_____

_____

SKELETONS AND ZOMBIES

Read about skeletons and zombies. Then use the facts and the Venn diagram to compare and contrast their traits.

Skeletons like to travel in mobs. They will burn in sunlight and try to stay in the shade as much as they can. However, a skeleton will be protected if it is wearing a helmet. Skeletons drop bones and arrows. They cannot see through glass. Skeletons are hard to defeat.

Zombies are often found in mobs. Sunlight can kill a zombie but a helmet will protect it. Zombies drop rotten flesh, carrots, and potatoes. Zombies are very slow, so it is easy to defeat them. Zombies are unable to see through glass.

FACTS

SKELETONS

Travel in mobs

Are burned by sunlight

Hard to defeat

Drop bones and arrows

Are protected by helmets

ZOMBIES

Travel in mobs

Are burned by sunlight

Easy to defeat

Drop rotten flesh, carrots, and potatoes

Are protected by helmets

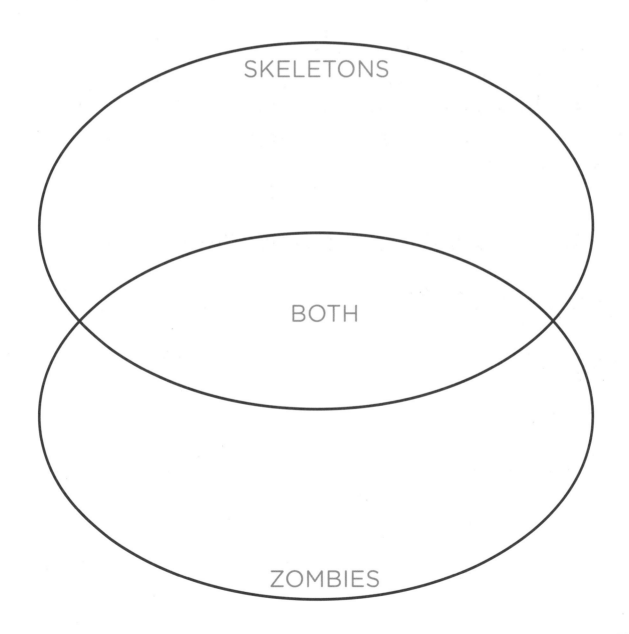

SKELETONS

BOTH

ZOMBIES

STEVE'S GARDEN

Read about Steve's garden.
Then number the events in the story in the order in which they happened.

Steve will need food. The best way to get food is to grow a garden. First Steve needs to make a hoe. Then he clears a flat spot for his garden. He collects seeds. Next, he tills the soil with his hoe and plants the seeds. Then he digs a hole in the ground for water. He pours water into the hole with a bucket. The garden needs lots of light. He puts a torch next to his crops. The torch will also keep monsters away.

_____ Steve clears a flat spot for his garden.

_____ Steve collects seeds.

_____ Steve digs a hole for water.

_____ Steve makes a hoe.

_____ Steve puts a torch next to his crops.

_____ Steve plants the seeds.

ALEX AND HER DIAMOND ARMOR

Read the story about Alex.
Then fill out the chart on the next page.

Alex is wearing her diamond armor. It is

the strongest armor of all. Alex needed 24

diamonds to make her set of armor. She needed

5 diamonds to make her helmet. She needed

8 diamonds to make her chestplate. To make

leggings she needed 7 diamonds. Her boots were

made with 4 diamonds. With her diamond armor

and sword, Alex can do anything! She might save

a village or destroy a mob. Watch out!

Diamonds Needed to Make Alex's Armor

Piece of Armor	Number of Diamonds
TOTAL	

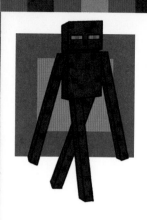

THE ENDERMAN

Read about Endermen. Then define the bolded words on the next page.

Hint: The answers are in the story.

An Enderman is tall and skinny with long arms. It is black and has creepy pink eyes. An Enderman is not dangerous but it does like to cause mischief (trouble). It takes blocks that players have put down and moves them to other places. It can also teleport, which means it can move itself in an instant. Enderman will spawn—or multiply—in darkness. It is harmed by water. Never stare at an Enderman because it will turn hostile, or mean.

Word	Meaning
Mischief	
Teleport	
Spawn	
Hostile	

Bonus: How did the story give you clues to what the words mean?

WHAT ARE IGLOOS?

Read about igloos.
Then answer the questions on the next page.

Igloos make a great pit stop if you are traveling.

You will find them in cold, snowy biomes—like

the Ice Plains and Cold Taiga. If you get cold or

hungry, you should find an empty igloo. Inside

will be a cozy room with everything you need.

It will have a rug, a crafting table, a torch, and a

heater. It will have lots of food stored on a shelf.

You will also find blankets and warm clothes.

Just watch out for polar bears!

What is the main idea of this text?

List three details that support the main idea.

1.

2.

3.

THE CAT IN THE JUNGLE

Read the story about the cat in the jungle.
Then answer the questions on the next page.

Will gazed at the trees stretching toward the sky. They were getting taller now. Thicker, too, and covered with lush green vines. *I made it!* thought Will. A shiver of excitement ran down his spine.

"Stop!" Mina suddenly whispered.

Will whirled around, expecting to come face to face with a monster. Instead, Mina was pointing at . . .

"A cat?" asked Will. He could barely see the spotted cat prowling in the thicket of trees.

"Not yet," Mina whispered. "He's an ocelot now—a wild cat. But if I feed him a little fish, I might be able to tame him."

"You have fish?" asked Will. His mouth watered at the thought.

From <u>Lost in the Jungle: Secrets of an Overworld Survivor</u> by Greyson Mann, Sky Pony Press, 2017.

What clues tell you that Will and Mina are walking deeper into a jungle?

_____

_____

_____

_____

How does Will feel about the jungle?

_____

_____

_____

_____

Which character seems to know more about the jungle? Use proof from the story.

_____

_____

_____

_____

How can you tell that Will is hungry?

_____

_____

_____

_____

ANSWER KEY

PAGE 294

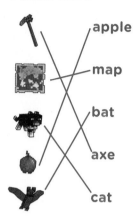

apple

map

bat

axe

cat

PAGE 295

1. apple
2. bat
3. map
4. cat
5. axe

PAGE 296

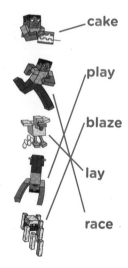

cake

play

blaze

lay

race

PAGE 297

1. cake
2. blaze
3. race
4. lay
5. play

PAGE 298

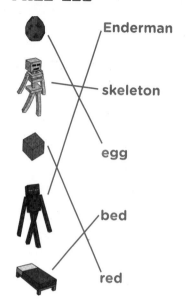

Enderman

skeleton

egg

bed

red

PAGE 299

1. egg
2. red
3. skeleton
4. bed
5. Enderman

PAGE 300

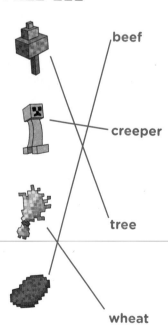

beef

creeper

tree

wheat

she

PAGE 301

1. wheat
2. beef
3. creeper
4. tree
5. she

PAGE 302

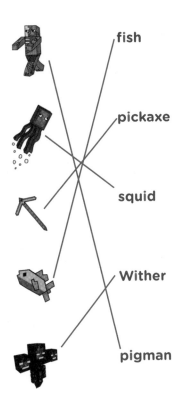

fish

pickaxe

squid

Wither

pigman

PAGE 303

1. pigman
2. pickaxe
3. squid
4. Wither
5. fish

PAGE 304

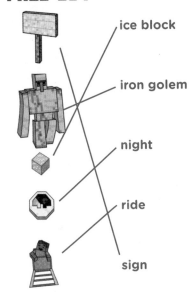

ice block

iron golem

night

ride

sign

PAGE 305

1. ice blocks
2. iron golem
3. sign
4. night
5. ride

PAGE 306

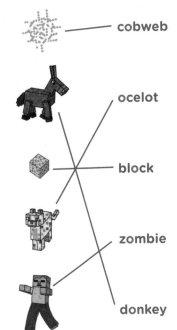

cobweb

ocelot

block

zombie

donkey

PAGE 307

1. ocelot
2. blocks
3. zombie
4. cobwebs
5. donkey

PAGE 308

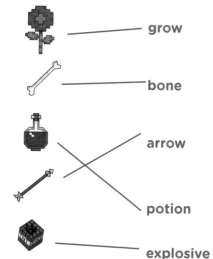

— grow

— bone

— arrow

— potion

— explosive

PAGE 309

1. grow
2. bone
3. potion
4. arrow
5. explosive

PAGE 310

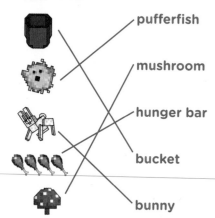

— pufferfish

— mushroom

— hunger bar

— bucket

— bunny

PAGE 311

1. bunny
2. bucket
3. hunger bar
4. pufferfish
5. mushrooms

PAGE 312

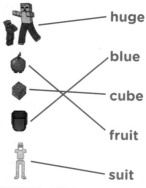

— huge

— blue

— cube

— fruit

— suit

PAGE 313

1. blue
2. cube
3. suit
4. fruit
5. huge

PAGES 314–315

1. The green creepers dance.

2. The player crafts an iron sword.

3. Alex fills the open chest.

4. The baby zombie rides a chicken.

5. The skeleton shoots a sharp arrow.

PAGE 316–317

Pig spawn on sandstone.	False
Pigs live in the Overworld.	True
Pigs like water.	False
A piglet is an adult pig.	False
Piglets grow into pigs in twenty minutes.	True

PAGES 318–319

The wolf's fur is ... — gray

A wild wolf has .... — red eyes

A mean wolf has .... — black eyes

A tame wolf has .... — a red collar

PAGES 320–321

What color are the cow's spots?

The cow's spots are **gray**.

How do cows walk?

Cows walk **slowly**.

What does a cow follow?

A cow follows **wheat**.

PAGES 320–321 *(CONTINUED)*

What do you need to milk a cow?

You need a **bucket** to milk a cow.

PAGES 322–323

The horse comes in **seven** colors.

The horse likes eating carrots because they are **crunchy**.

A **saddle** lets you ride the horse.

When a horse is tame, it shows **hearts**.

PAGES 324–325

Zombies are

❑ Fast ☒ Slow ❑ Quiet

What kind of sounds do zombies make?

❑ Moaning ❑ Screaming ☒ Groaning

What can kill a zombie?

☒ Sunlight ❑ Darkness ❑ Other zombies

Who can a zombie call for help?

❑ Wolves ☒ Other zombies ❑ Dragons

If a zombie attacks you, it can turn you into a

❑ Robot ☒ Zombie ❑ Zombie robot

PAGES 326–327

Creepers can sneak up on you because they are **very quiet**.

Creepers might be hiding in a **cave**.

If they **explode**, you could be harmed.

Creepers have a fear of **cats**.

Creepers can't open doors, but they can climb **ladders**.

PAGES 328–329

The Ender Dragon is a **boss** mob.

The dragon lives in **the End**.

The dragon flies in **circles** in the sky.

The balls of fire are **purple**.

To get an egg from an Ender Dragon, you have to **destroy** it.

PAGES 330–331

What is the main idea of this story?

The boats in the new version of Minecraft are better than the boats in the old version.

Give three details to support the main idea:

*Note: answer may vary, but should include 3 of the 4 details below

1. *The new boats are stronger and don't break apart so easily.*
2. *The new boats come with paddles*
3. *The new boats go faster than the old boats.*
4. *The new boats can carry more people.*

PAGES 332–333

The ghast:
B. Floated

The ghast was:
C. Sad

The ghast's mouth and eyes are:
B. Black

The ghast shot:
A. Fireballs

The arrow almost hit the ghast's:
C. Legs

PAGES 334–335

Potion Colors and Their Effects

COLOR	EFFECT
Green	**Jump high**
Blue	**See at night**
Purple	**Restore health**
Red	**Strength**
Yellow	**Health boost**
Orange	**Fire protection**

PAGES 336–337

What is the cause of the mother's anger?

Steve ate all of his birthday cake after she told him not to eat any of it.

What is the effect of the mother's anger?

Steve has to call his friends to tell them his birthday party is cancelled.

PAGES 338-339

SKELETONS
Hard to defeat
Drop bones and arrows

Travel in mobs
Burned by daylight
Protected by helmet
BOTH

Easy to defeat
Drop rotten flesh, carrots, potatoes

ZOMBIES

PAGES 340-341

2   Steve clears a flat spot for his garden.
3   Steve collects seeds.
5   Steve digs a hole for water.
1   Steve makes a hoe.
6   Steve puts a torch next to his crops.
4   Steve plants the seeds.

PAGES 342-343

Piece of Armor	Number of Diamonds
Helmet	5
Chestplate	8
Leggings	7
Boots	4
TOTAL	24

PAGES 344-345

Word	Meaning
Mischief	**Trouble**
Teleport	**Move in an instant**
Spawn	**Multiply**
Hostile	**Mean**

PAGES 344-345 (CONTINUED)

Bonus: The different ways definitions are given are by
 1) using the definition in parentheses (trouble),
2) using the phrase "which means" after the word and before the definition,
3) using dashes—such as these—to explain the definition, and
4) using a comma and the word "or" before the definition.

PAGES 346-347

Note: Answers may vary. This is a sample of possible answers.
What is the main idea of this text?
The main idea of the text is that an igloo makes a good pit stop if you are in a snowy biome and get cold or hungry.

List three details that support the main idea.
1. Igloos have everything you need.
2. Igloos have food stored on shelves.
3. Igloos have blankets and warm clothes

PAGES 348-349

What clues show that Will and Mina are deeper into the jungle?
The clues are that the trees were getting taller, thicker, and covered with lush green vines.

How does Will feel about the jungle?
Excited and/or nervous.

Which character seems to know more about the jungle? Use proof from the story?
Mina seems to know more because she isn't as nervous and she knows that the ocelot is not a cat.

How can you tell that Will is hungry?
His mouth waters at the thought of fish.

WANT TO BATTLE THE SUMMER SLIDE?

Try this workbook for more learning adventures.

SUMMER BRIDGE LEARNING FOR MINECRAFTERS

BRIDGING GRADES 1 to 2

ALIGNS WITH NATIONAL COMMON CORE STANDARDS

NANCY ROGERS BOSSE
ILLUSTRATED BY BILL GREENHEAD